Seeking Strength and Joy

POEMS, PHOTOGRAPHY & MEDITATIONS
INSPIRED BY JESUS

Text copyright © 2023 Bethan Bennett
Photography © 2023 Bethan Bennett

The right of Bethan Bennett to be identified as the author and photographer of this work has been asserted by her in accordance with the Copyright, Designs and Patents Act 1988.

All rights reserved. No part of this publication may be reproduced or transmitted in any form or by any means, electronic or mechanical, including photocopy, recording or any information storage and retrieval system, without permission in writing from the publisher.

Published by Bethan Bennett
For permission requests, contact Bethan: bethanbennett@icloud.com

First edition 2023

Scripture quotations marked NLT are taken from the *Holy Bible,* New Living Translation, copyright © 1996, 2004. Used by permission of Tyndale House Publishers, Inc., Wheaton, Illinois 60189. All rights reserved.

Scripture quotations marked NIV taken from the Holy Bible, New International Version Anglicised. Copyright © 1979, 1984, 2011 Biblica, formerly International Bible Society. Used by permission of Hodder & Stoughton Ltd, an Hachette UK company. All rights reserved. "NIV" is a registered trademark of Biblica. UK trademark 1448790.

In memory of my gran, who always inspired and encouraged me in my creativity when growing up; gifting me my first journal that allowed me to process my thoughts and sparked a love of writing. Her own words of praise to her Lord and Saviour uplifting my soul in a time of trouble. Thank you!

Contents

Introduction..1

Part One - Praise & Worship...................5
Part Two - Strength & Joy.......................27
Part Three - Truth & Creativity..............71

Final Words...104
Acknowledgements................................105
About the Author......................................106

Introduction

"Cast your cares on the Lord and he will sustain you; he will never let the righteous be shaken."
-Psalm 55:22 NIV

When I read this verse as an exhausted mum of two - squeezing in some quiet time before the little ones woke for the day - little did I know the impact it would have on the foreseeable future.

The months leading up to that morning quiet time had been quite an adjustment for my family and me. We moved house into a home that wouldn't feel like home for quite some time, welcomed a new baby to our family and were adjusting to new work patterns.

As a mum of two under two I was exhausted and overwhelmed. It was at this point that I started to set an alarm to get up and spend some time with Jesus before my little boys woke up ready to start the day.

As I read Psalm 55:22 one morning, it filled my heart with such hope and soon became my 'go-to' verse every morning; I would recite it at the start of each day, giving my cares and worries over to the Lord. I was greatly encouraged that when I took my worries and concerns to the Lord, he would give me the strength I needed to get through the day when I felt utterly depleted.

Fast forward a year or so, after delving into the Psalms where I discovered so many verses about God being our strength, our refuge and our help in times of trouble, I read these words:

'The Lord is good, a refuge in time of trouble. He cares for those who trust in Him.'
-Nahum 1: 7 NIV

When I read this verse I thought I was reading the words of a Psalm, so was surprised to discover it was in fact, from a different book of the Bible.

Reading that verse in Nahum that morning reminded me how often this sentiment appears in the word of God – 43 times in the book of Psalms alone.

As I had that thought, two things struck me.
1. These words of comfort are not just a nice sentiment to promote positive thinking but are solid truth that we can cling on to and help us stand firm in our faith.
2. As Christians, we're never promised a trouble-free life but we are promised that God will be present in our trouble, that He will be our refuge and our rock.

King David, who wrote many of the Psalms, was no stranger to suffering and hardship himself. While he certainly enjoyed positions of high power and defeated a giant with just a stone and sling, he also faced life's storms – he spent a lot of time on the run hiding from a man who wanted to take his life, and he committed adultery and murder. David was not perfect. But he did know how to seek God as his strength and look to Him for comfort and refuge; and that, I admire.

It's so easy to worship God when things are going well and we feel we are winning at life. But what about those times when everything goes to pot? It's not so easy to sing praise and worship to God. We often turn to the things of this world to satisfy our longings; a takeaway meal when we're exhausted at the end of the day, an impulse purchase from our favourite online shop or an evening spent on the sofa binge watching the next show on our list of things to watch. Only, we find we are not deeply satisfied by these things. They may offer us temporary relief but these things do not bring us strength, nor do they bring us lasting joy. That, can only come from Jesus.

In my times of desperation and overwhelm, I leaned on God and found immense strength and joy. During these times I found myself pouring my heart out to Jesus, writing poems of praise but also pleas for Jesus to strengthen me, for Him to be my refuge and my strength.

I have always loved writing, journalling and photography; experiencing God through the pen on the paper or the camera set up to capture a stunning sunset. My heart cannot help but stop and worship the creator of this beautiful world. Words would come into my head and form short poems evoked by the experience I was having; An experience of connecting to God and praising Him for the beauty He has created.

When I found myself reading the poems I'd written and using them as prayers during my quiet time with Jesus, I knew I had to compile them in one place. And so this book was born - a compilation of photography and poetry inspiring praise and worship to Jesus and seeking strength and joy from Him.

I pray that you will read these poems, take in the scriptures, marvel at our Creator through the photography and be inspired to find strength and joy in Him alone.

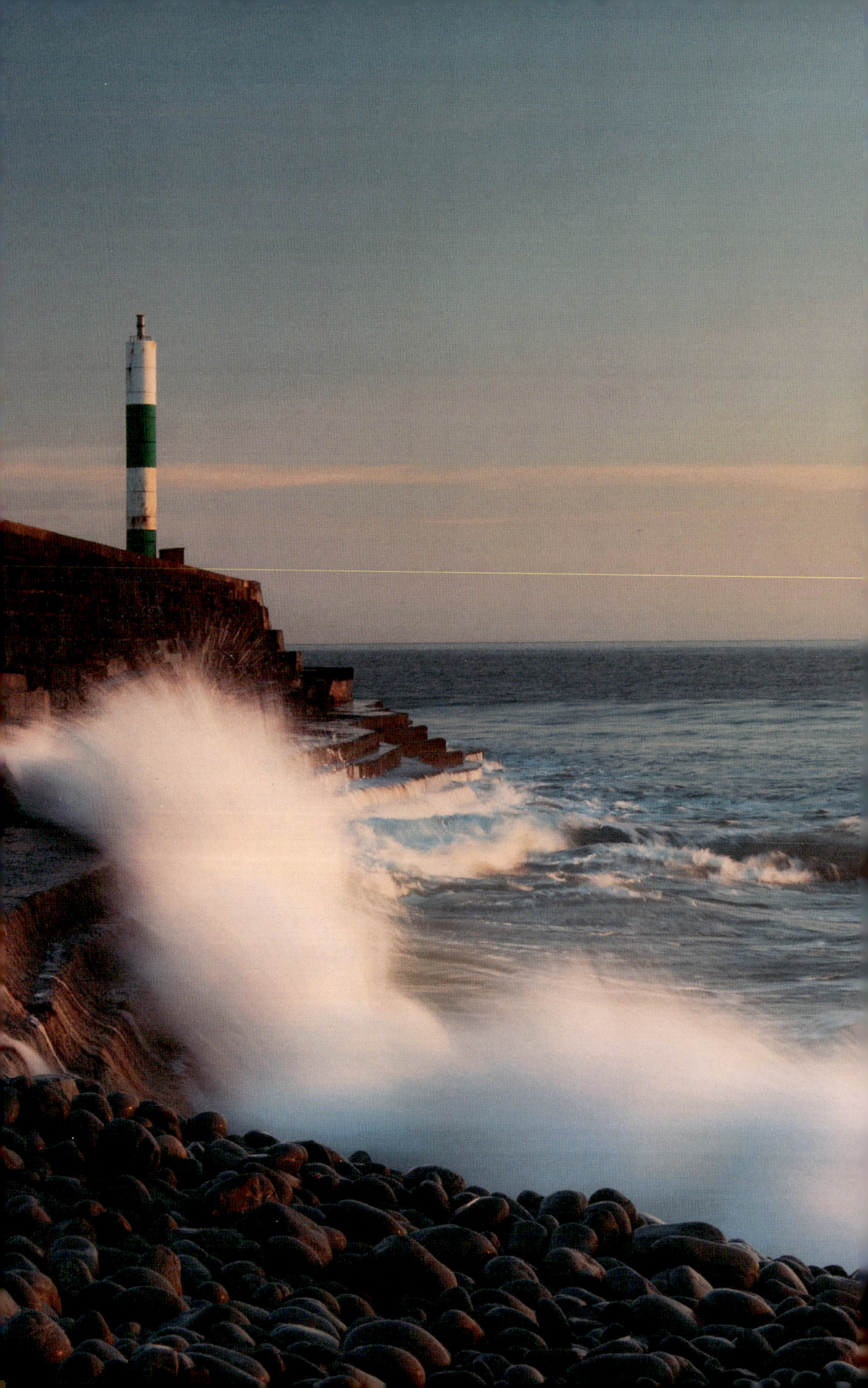

Part One
Praise & Worship

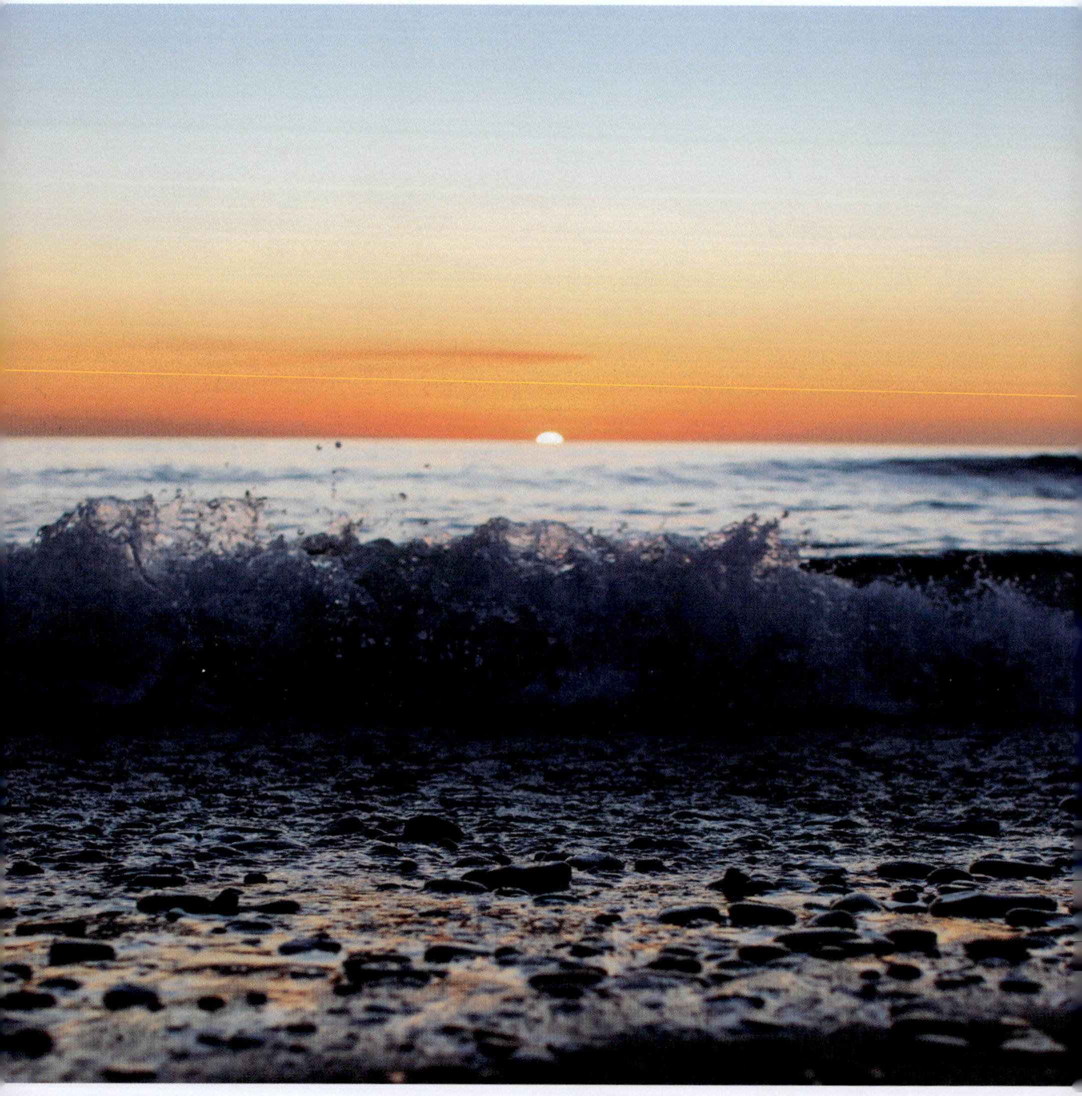

He is Worthy of Praise

Psalm 103 has always been one of my favourite Psalms; it starts with David instructing his soul to sing praises to God.

Praise the Lord, my soul;
all my inmost being, praise his holy name.
Praise the Lord, my soul,
and forget not all his benefits.
-Psalm 103:1-2 NIV

What I love about this Psalm is how descriptive David is in telling of the goodness of God; He praises the Lord for all he has done. Whilst Psalm 103 is one of my favourites, it is not the only example we have of people writing their praises to the Lord. In fact, in so many of the Psalms we see people praising God. What strikes me however, is that a lot of these psalms of praise appear to be written when people are in a state of anguish and despair. In Psalm 62 and 63 we see David earnestly seeking God. David is being assaulted, he knows people are pursuing him to kill him, and he longs to be close to God. Yet, he states that he will praise God for as long as he lives; he will always sing glory to God. Despite David's circumstances being less than ideal, he turns his heart to worship God. I think we can learn a lot from David.

I truly believe that praising God and stating the good things He has done, strengthens our relationship with and faith in Him – even in the hard times.

The following poems are my songs of praise to Jesus; me turning my heart to worship the God of the universe.

01

O Jesus, I praise you for glorious sunshine that reveals the beauty in your creation.

O Jesus, I praise you for rain that brings refreshment.

I praise you, Jesus, for coming to earth as a babe to show us the way in which we should live.

I praise you, Jesus, for the sacrifice you made so we can be in eternal relationship with you.

You long to be in relationship with us more than anything.

Who am I that you are mindful of me?
I am not worthy but because of you, Jesus, I am.

Your grace is enough.

Without it we would be a mess.

You make us complete.

You make us your creation.

*When I consider your heavens,
the work of your fingers,
the moon and the stars,
which you have set in place,
what is mankind
that you are mindful of them,
human beings that you care for them?
-Psalm 8:3-4 NIV*

02

The whole earth is filled with awe at your wonders.
How wonderful you are!

You make the sunshine rise and set
and do so in the most unique and spectacular way.
You cover the sky in a magnificent blanket of silver gems.
You create the Red Kite with its 'V' shaped tail, to circle the sky.
This is your nature.

You create me in your image.
You provide my every need.
You are good.
You are faithful.
You are love.
This is your nature.

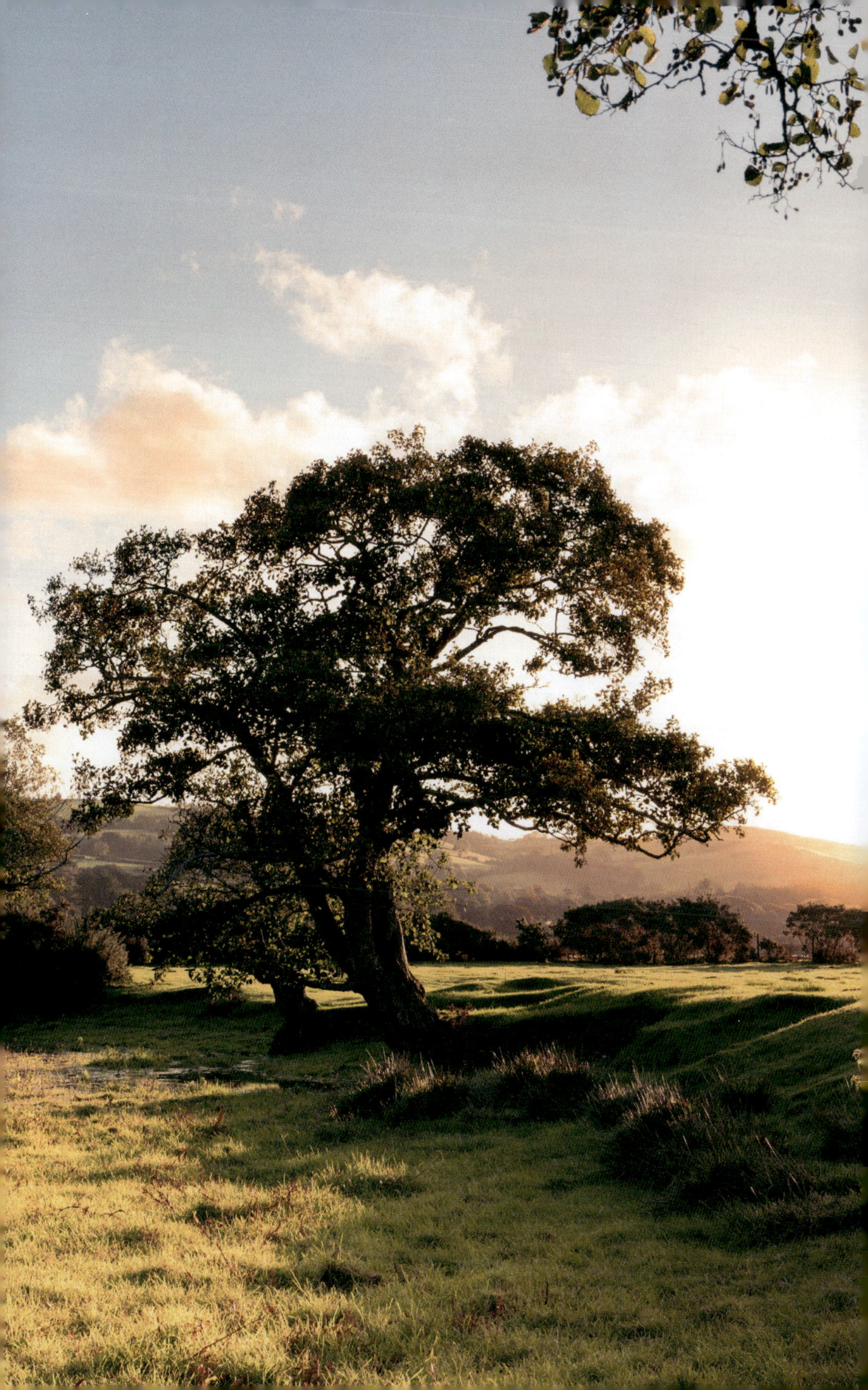

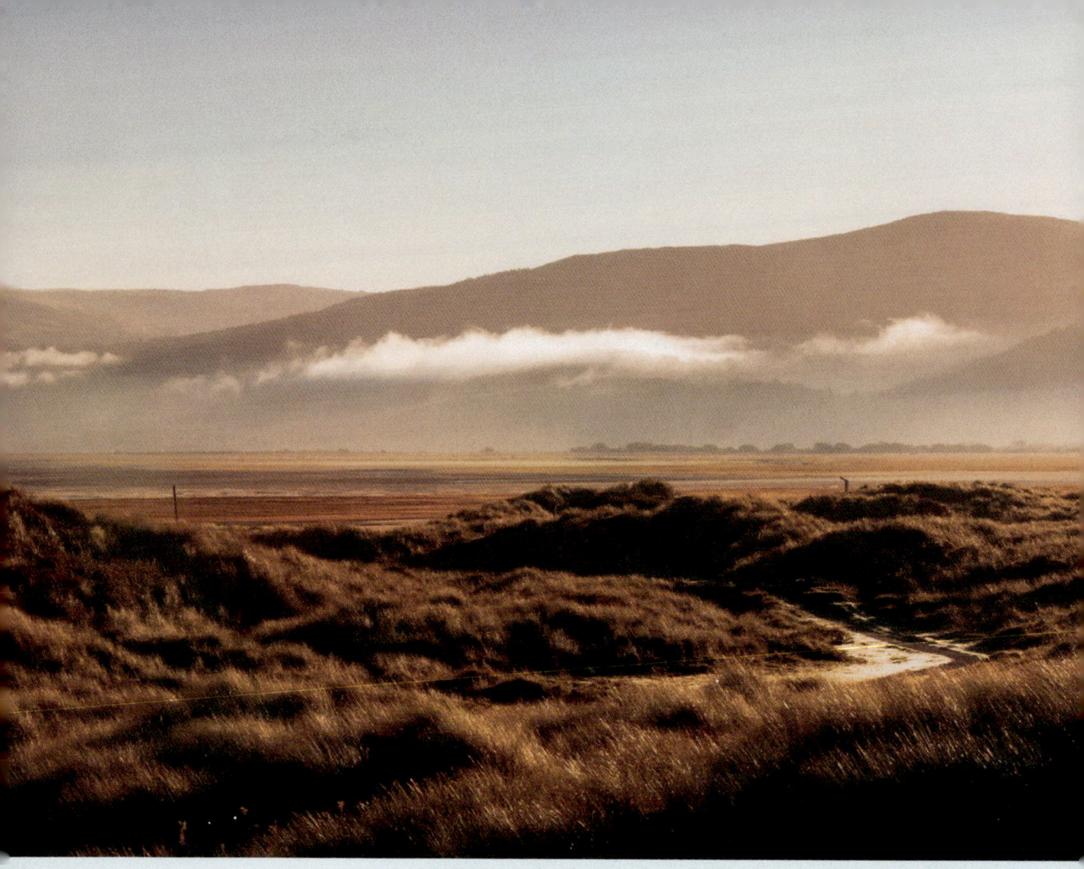
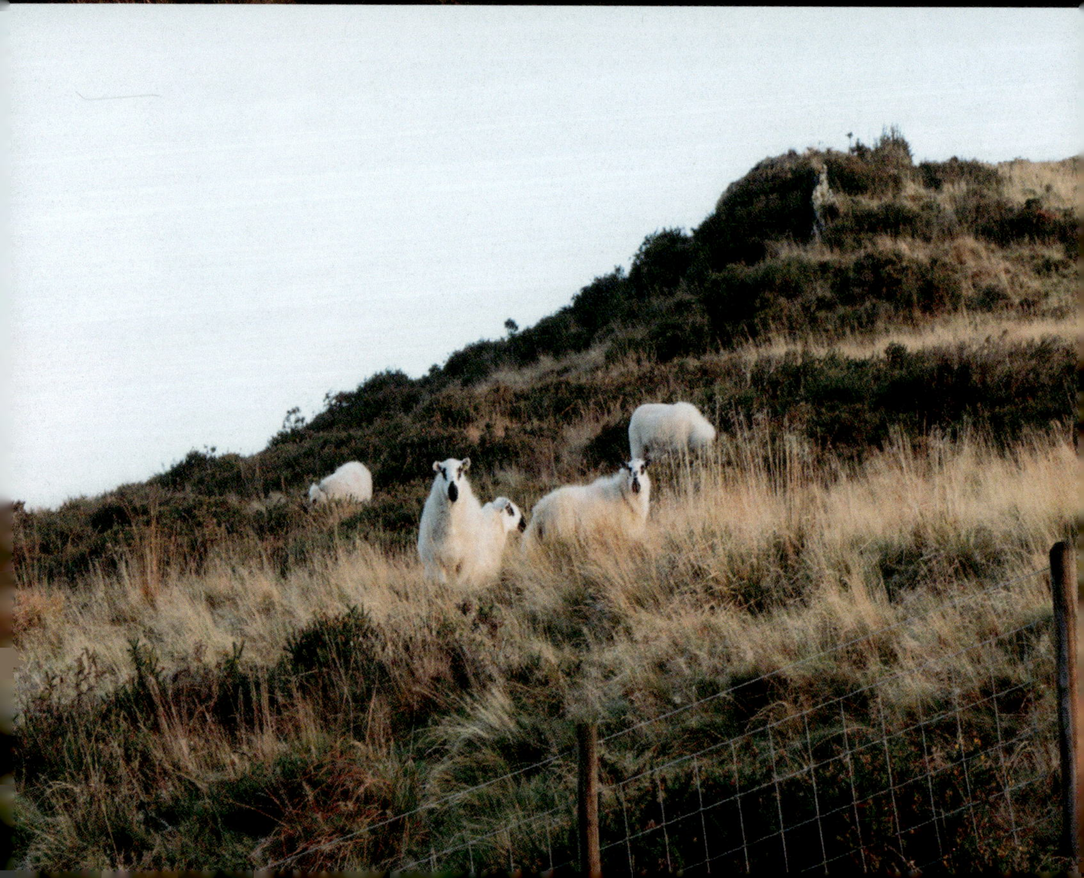

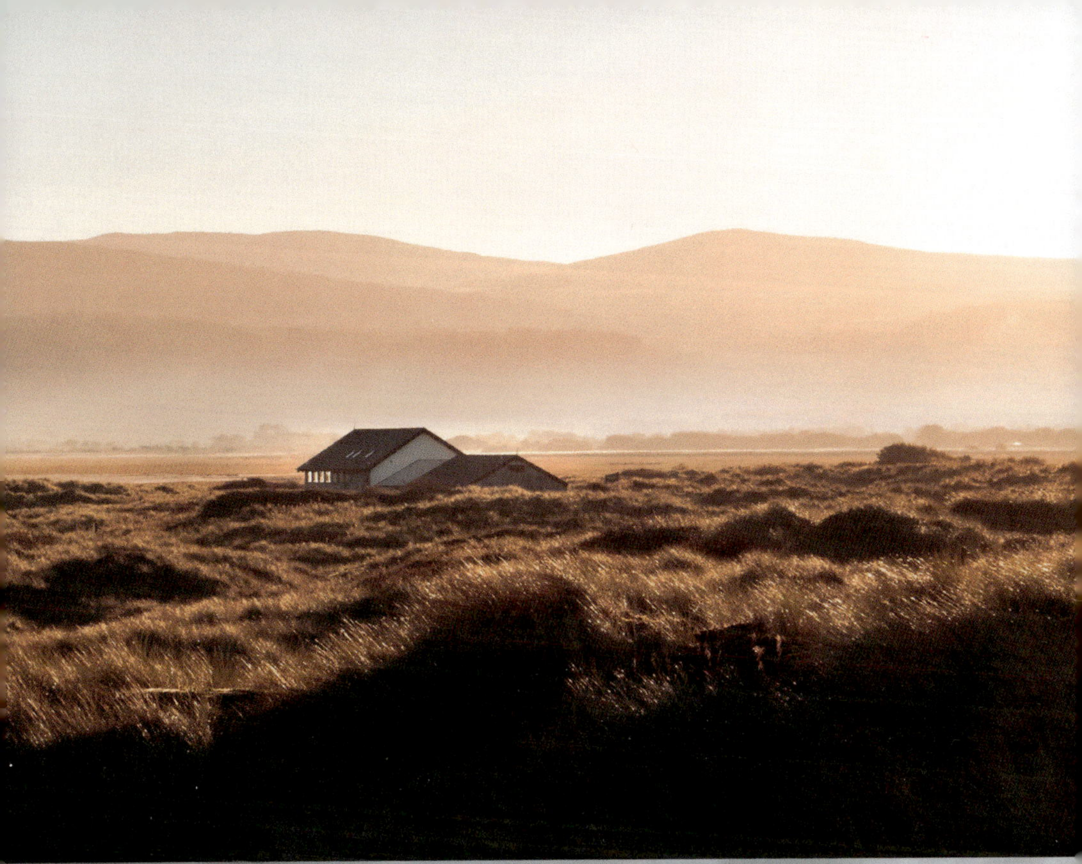
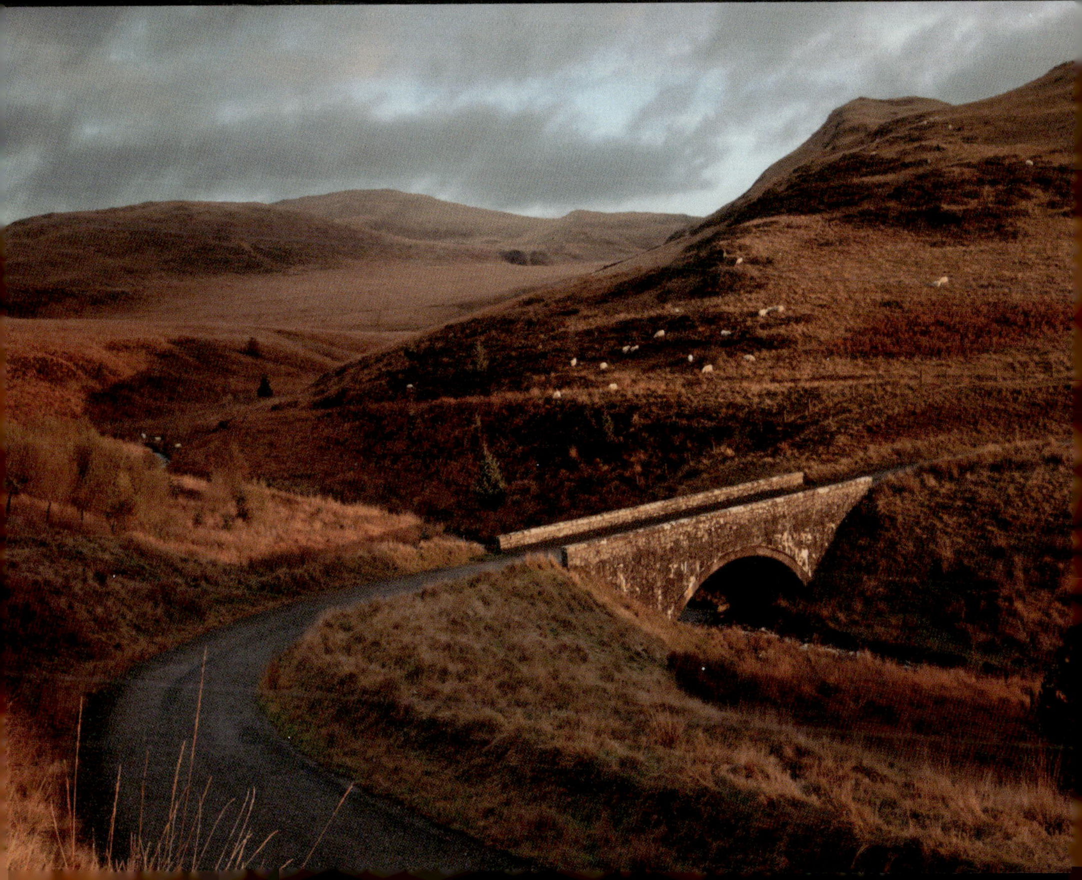

03

Lord, Lord, how majestic is your name.
Out of nothing you created the universe.
You placed each star in the sky;
You paint the sky each morning and evening;
You control the tide with a silver ball in the sky.
Through Moses, you parted the sea.
Through David, you defeated a giant.
Through Jesus, you give us eternal life.

Lord, Lord, how majestic is your name.
I praise you.
Because of your mercy, we can boldly approach you.
Because of your grace, we can have direct contact with you;
the master of the universe.

Let us not forget your wonderful works.
Let us not grow complacent at your wonder.
Lord, Lord, how majestic is your name.

Let all that I am praise the Lord;
may I never forget the good things he does for me.
-Psalm 103: 2 NLT

04

O, Jesus, I praise your name.
My whole being praises your Holy name.
Be thankful to the Lord and shout about his goodness from the rooftops.

Thank you Jesus, for the world around me;
for your beautiful creation.
I praise you for the way raindrops cling to a spider's web;
the way dew drops sparkle like gems in the magical morning light.
I see you in the evening sky when the sun begins to go down on another day.
I praise you for the way you paint the sky in the most magnificent shades of pink, orange, yellow, purple and blue.
Seedlings sprouting and growing make my heart sing.
They were once but a seed.
Now they are leaves and stems growing, preparing to flower.
Jesus, I praise you.

Father, you are good.
Jesus, you are good.
Holy Spirit, you are good.
You delight in only giving us good things.
May we proclaim your goodness and see your goodness in our day to day going about life.

Rejoice, my soul and see the wondrous works of your mighty saviour.
Seek him always.
Give him thanks always.
Praise him always.

Whatever is good and perfect is a gift coming down to us from God our Father, who created all the lights in the heavens.
-James 1:17 NLT

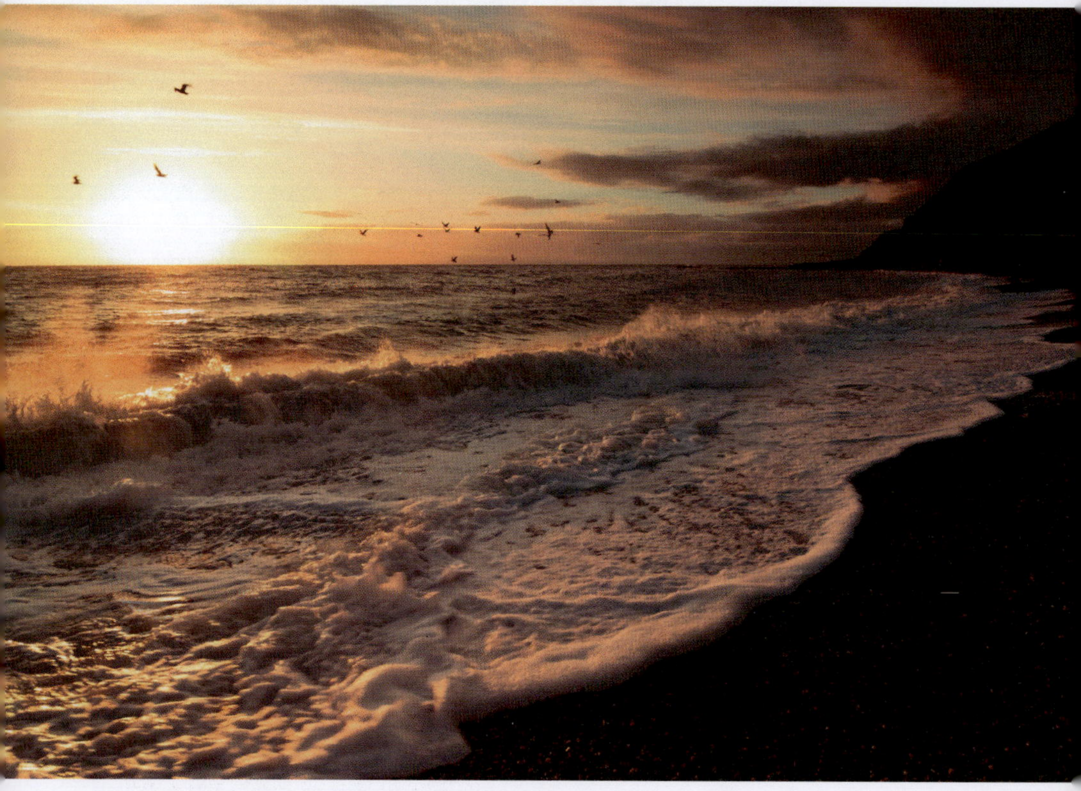

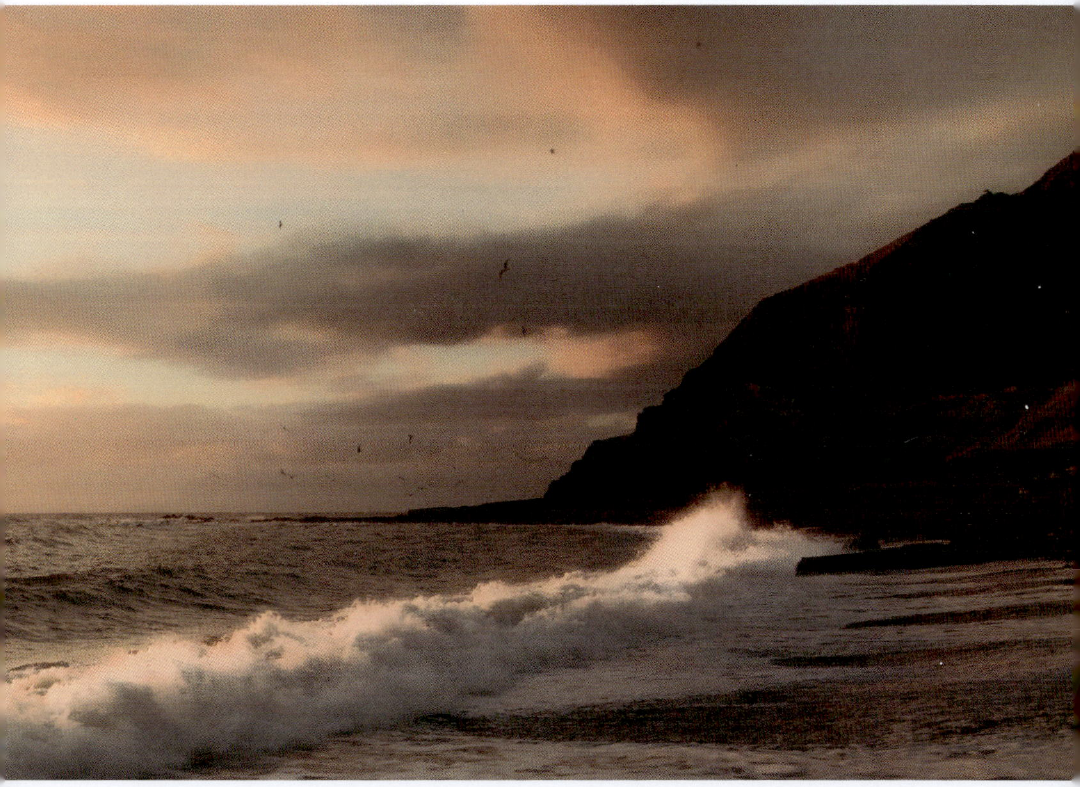

05

I sit. I sit and be still, willing my mind to be quiet.
My physical body is tired and I ask of the Lord to strengthen it.
My Lord, my Lord, how wonderful you are.

You give strength to the weary;
You give hope to the hopeless.
Lord, you are our guide.
You light up the way in which we should go.
You don't leave anyone behind and your plan always prevails.
Those who feel lost will find their way if they look to you.

By your grace, and your grace alone, those who call on your name will be saved.
How wonderful will that day be when every person, every creature bows down before the throne and declares, 'He is Lord'.

You are the Lord almighty;
The One who brought the universe into existence;
The One who placed the stars in the sky to shine;
The One who knows how many grains of sand are on the earth;
The One who made the mountains to reach the sky.
My Lord, my Lord, how wonderful is your name.

At the name of Jesus every knee should bow,
in heaven and on earth and under the earth,
and every tongue acknowledge that Jesus Christ is Lord,
to the glory of God the Father.
-Philippians 2:10-11 NIV

06

O, how my soul is full. Full of joy at a murmuration of starlings.
I marvel of God's wonderful creation.
How he crafted the dance of these golden flecked birds.

O, how my soul is full. Full of joy at the brilliant white of the waves.
The waves that come in and out, that ebb and flow.

O, how my soul is full. Full of joy at doing something I love.
Being creative;
Capturing the beauty that God made with his own hands.

I sit and marvel at how his creation knows no bounds.
I sit and am thankful that the creator of the world created me.
I sit and am thankful for the love of photography he so carefully crafted when creating me.

O, how my soul is full.

For you created my inmost being;
you knit me together in my mother's womb.
I praise you because I am fearfully and wonderfully made;
your works are wonderful,
I know that full well.
-Psalm 139:13-14 NIV

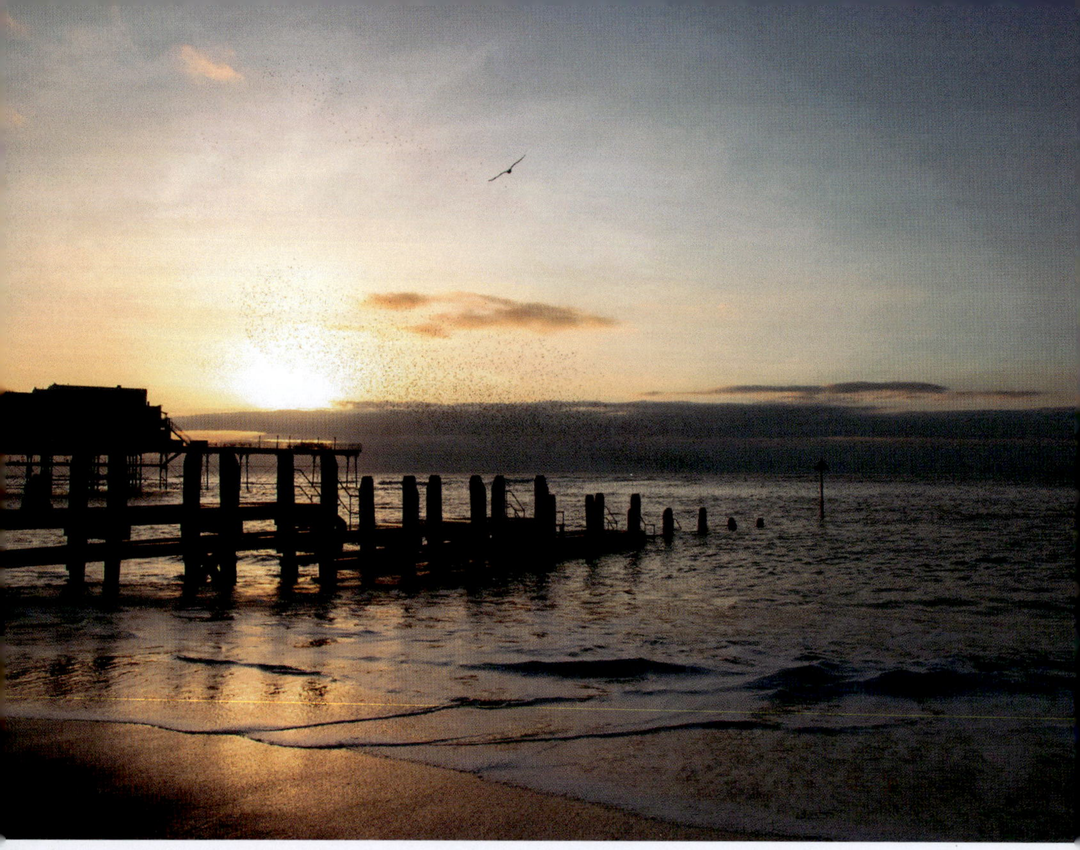

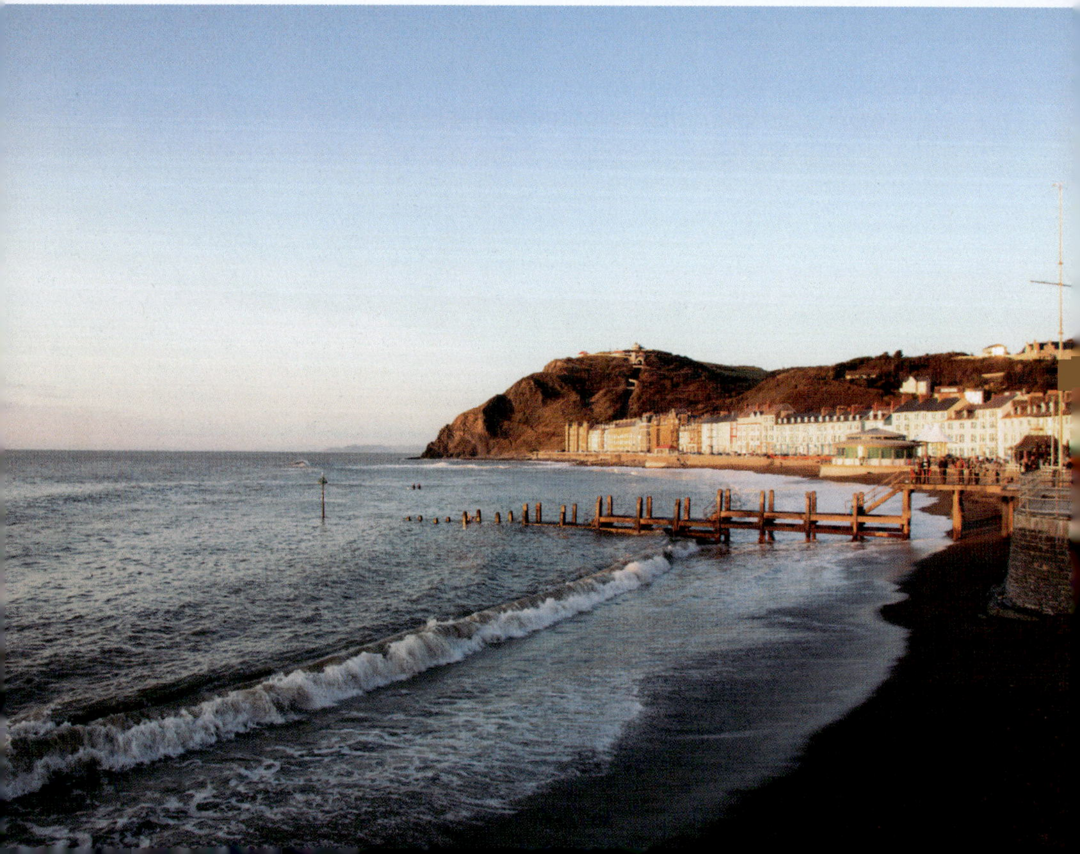

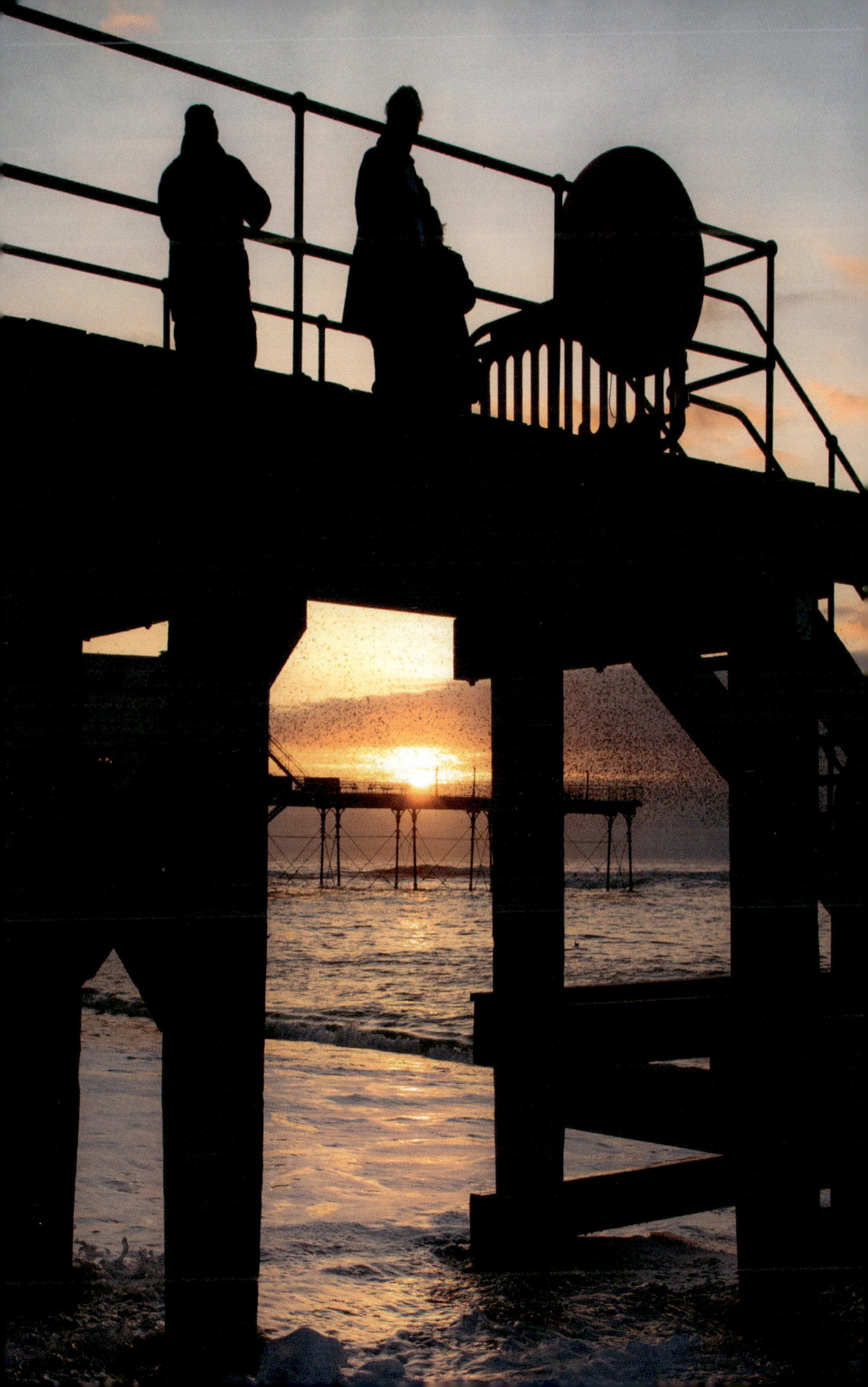

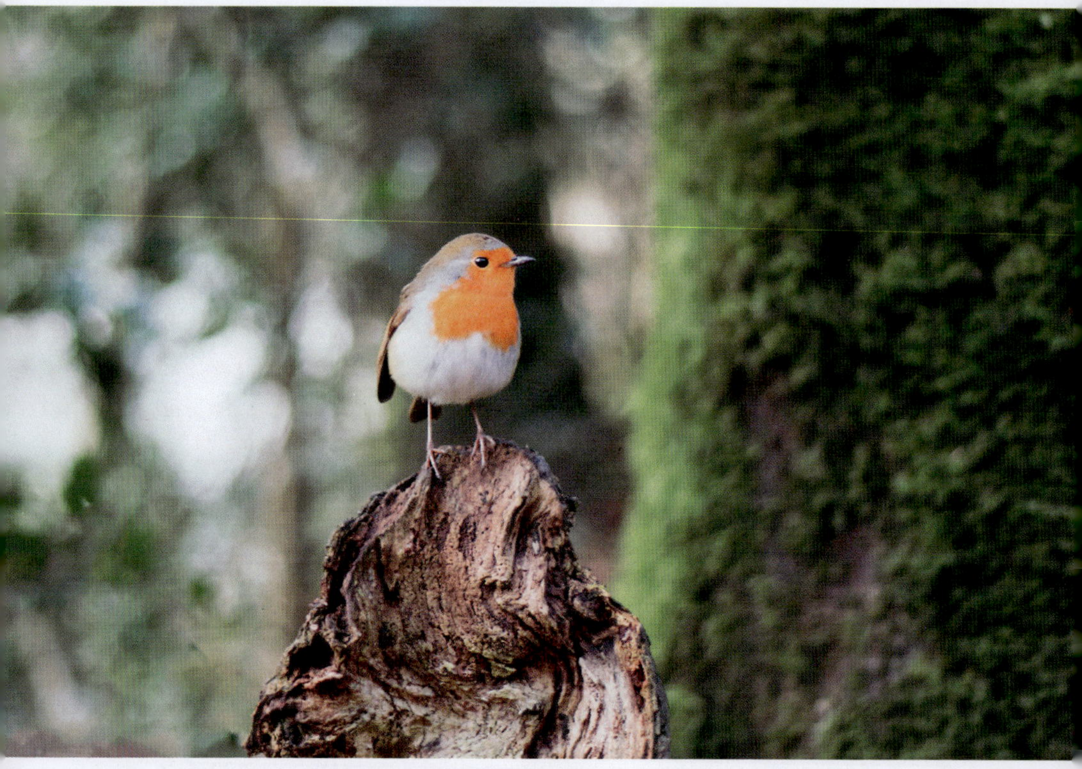

Part Two
Strength & Joy

Finding Strength and Joy in Jesus

Life is difficult.
I'm sure we can agree that we have all had our share of difficult situations to navigate and at times, just want to escape from it all and wish someone would just change the circumstances.

At times, I've certainly felt this way as I've adjusted to new family dynamics, new living situations and new working patterns. At times I felt at the end of my tether, I felt exhausted and just wanted something to change.

At the most difficult point, I started to prioritise spending time with Jesus so would get up before everyone else and read my bible.
It was then that I discovered verses about God being a refuge and our strength in times of trouble.

As time went on and I discovered more and more verses, I felt a lightness within me I had not felt in a long time. The more time I spent with Jesus, the more I found strength and Jesus filled me with joy.
I love that we can turn to Jesus in all things and at all times.
And we can do this boldy, with confidence.

How amazing is it that we can go to God, who sits on his heavenly throne, with confidence?

We can be bold in our approach to God. We need not be timid and shy.

Why? Because Jesus bridged the gap between God and man when he sacrificed his life on the cross. Because of God's mercy and grace, we find help in times of need.

This is exactly what happened to me. In times of need, I approached God and spoke honestly with Him.

My circumstances may not have changed but I certainly have.
Speaking out those verses each morning about God being our refuge and strength, seeking God first thing in the morning and giving over my cares and concerns to Him made the difficulties in my life much easier to deal with. Yes, it was still hard and no, I didn't always manage to get up before the rest of the house but my faith deepened, God gave me strength and I found refuge in Him.

The words that follow in this section of the book are honest, raw and vulnerable. They are from the heart and speak of the strength and joy I find in Jesus even when I'm in the deep deep valley.

So let us come boldly to the throne of our gracious God.
There we will receive his mercy, and we will find grace to help us when we
need it most.
-Hebrews 4:16 NLT

07

O, Holy Father, I praise you for I am fearfully and wonderfully made.
But, who am I that you would love me?

You made the majestic mountains and the roaring seas.
You made the sun to rule the day,
and the moon and starry host, the night.

Yet, it was humans, you chose to have a relationship with.
Us humans, for whom you sent your one and only son to die so that we may have eternal life;
Eternal life with you, the God of the universe.

How wonderful are you Lord.

Though this season is hard, I cling to your word.
You will deliver us.
You will sustain us.
You will give us rest.

Keep my mind focused on you.
Carry us, Jesus, through this life until it is time to come home.
May we work as though working for you and not for men.
May we be faithful in all we do, and in all we do, may we have integrity.

> *Work willingly at whatever you do, as though you were working for the Lord rather than for people.*
> *-Colossians 3:23 NLT*

08

I fix my eyes on you, Jesus;
I seek your face always;
For you are the Lord Almighty,
The God Eternal,
The Alpha and Omega.

When I'm tempted to look at my situations and focus on the imperfections, the muddiness and murkiness, I look up.
I fix my eyes on you and choose to see the beauty;
I choose to see you.

When I'm overwhelmed by the state of the planet
and despair at human actions, I look up.
I fix my eyes on you and choose to see your glory;
I choose to see your hand at work.

When my soul is tired and weary and my default mood is grumpy,
 I look up.
I fix my eyes on you and choose you as my strength and joy;
I choose to let you carry me through.

I fix my eyes on you, Jesus;
I seek your face always;
For you are the Lord Almighty,
The God Eternal,
The Alpha and Omega.

*Search for the Lord and for his strength;
continually seek him.
-Psalm 105:4 NLT*

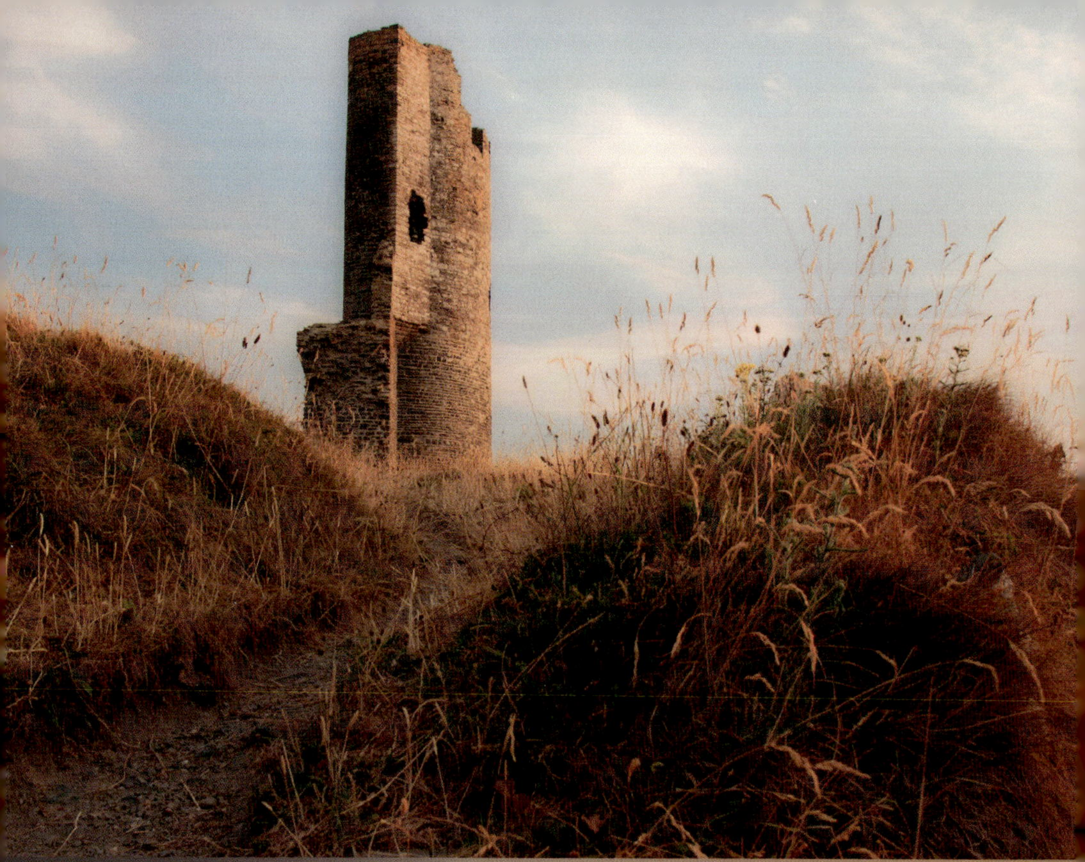

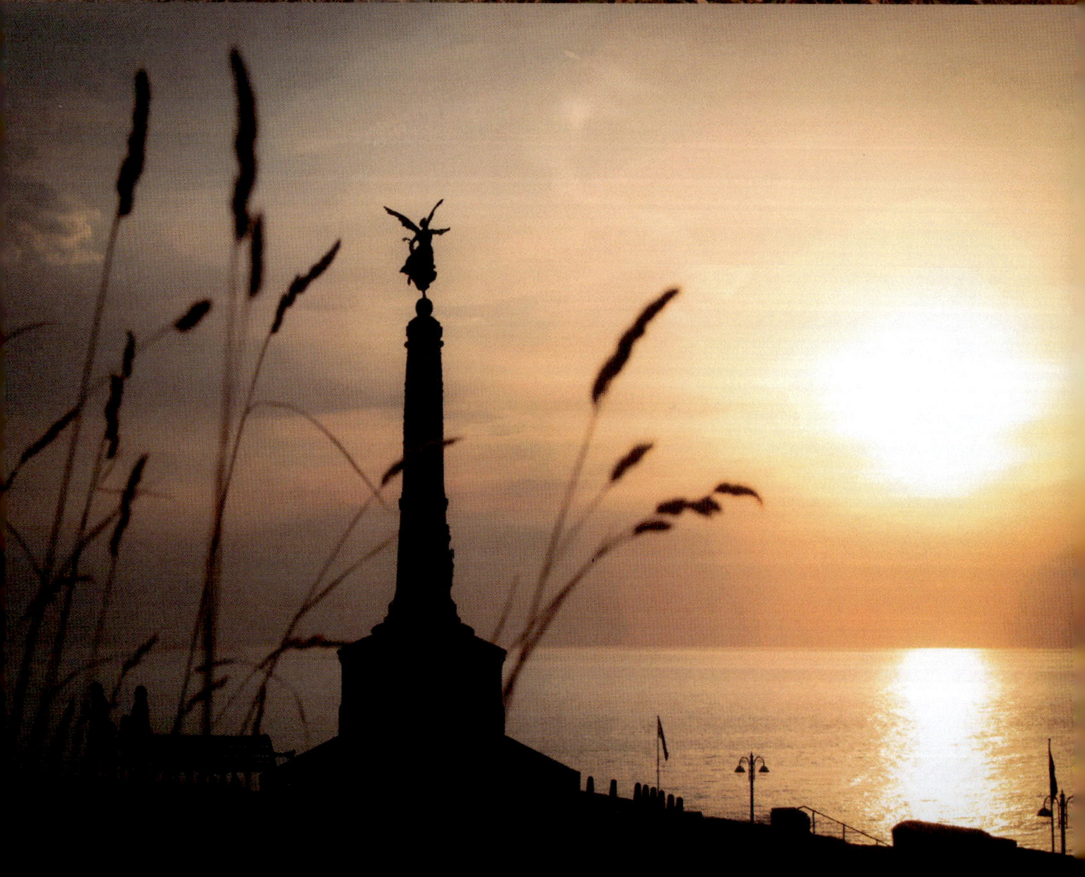

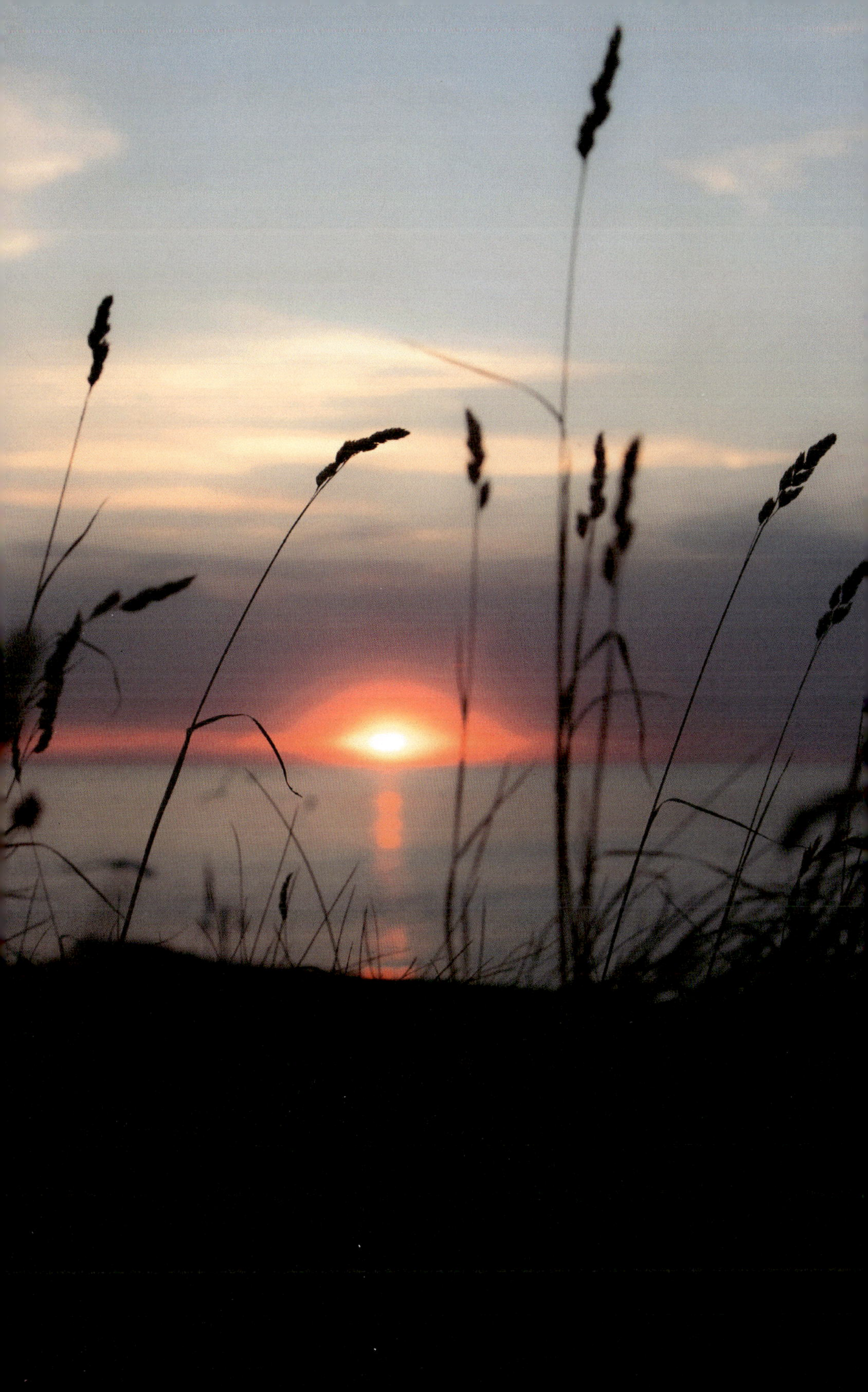

09

When my soul is downcast and depressed;
When I can't bare to get out of bed in the morning;
When I start the day with tears rolling down my cheeks;
You, O Lord, show me your beauty.
You, O Lord, show me your goodness.

In the golden sunshine contrasting with stormy grey clouds;
In the unique snowflakes that fall on my forest-surrounded cottage
In the whispers of love and encouragement to my soul;
In the pits of despair;
You, O Lord, show me that 'it is well.'

Then they cried out to the Lord in their trouble,
and he brought them out of their distress.
He stilled the storm to a whisper;
the waves of the sea were hushed.
-Psalm 107: 28-29 NIV

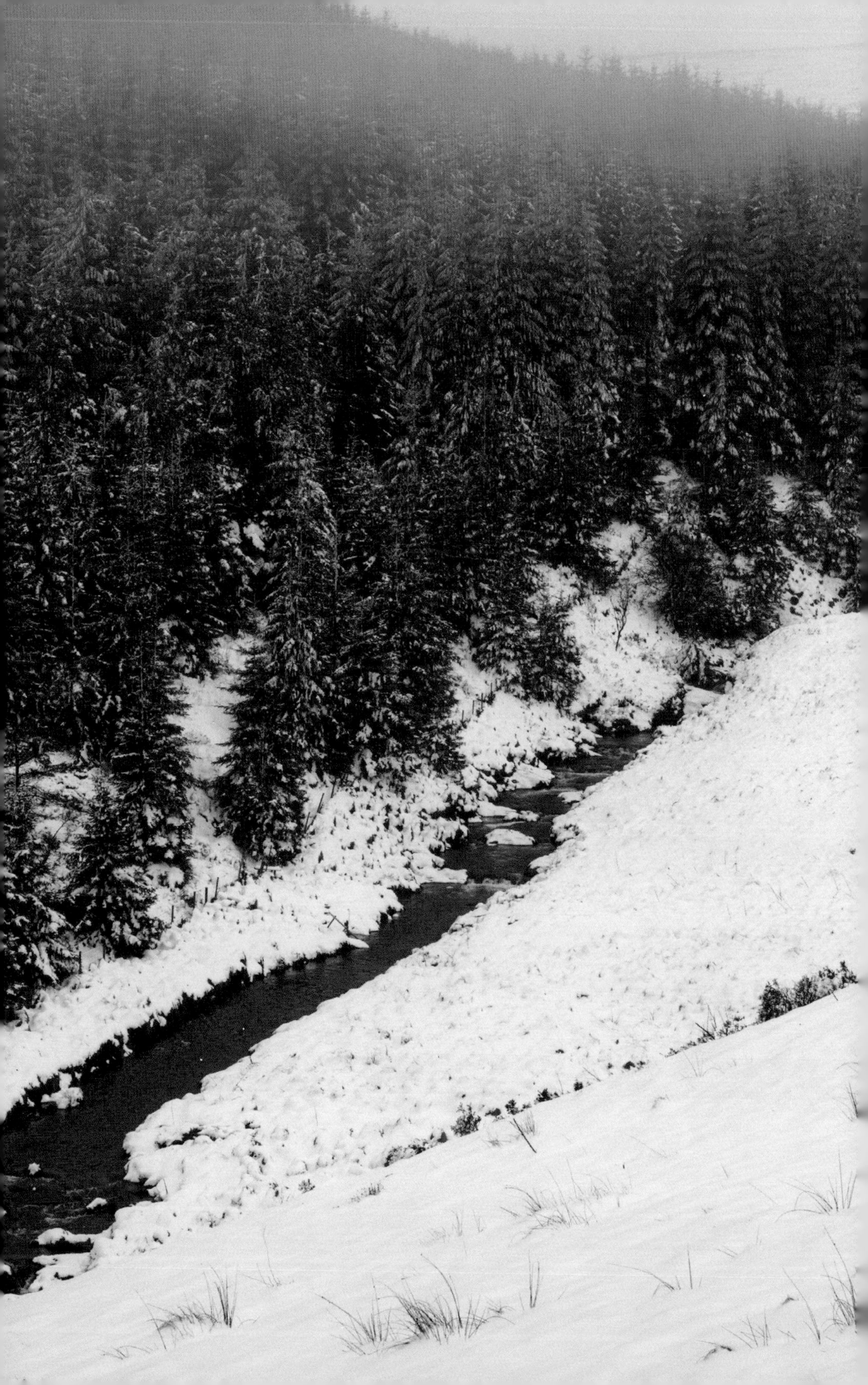

*I will praise the Lord at all times.
I will constantly speak his praises.*
-Psalm 34:1 NLT

10

O Lord, how I love you.
You give me strength when I need strength.
I sought you and found you.
My eyes are open to see you;
My ears are open to hear you.

You, Lord, truly are my refuge;
My strength in times of trouble.
You are where my hope comes from;
I put all my trust in you.

Your works are mighty but also simple.
It is in the little things that I see you.
It is in the gentle whispers that I hear you.
You are at work now and always.

May your praise always be on my lips.
May I always tell of your wondrous deeds.
May your love be known to the ends of the earth.

11

Jesus, I want to see you today.
I want to hear you today.
I want to draw close to you today.
Lord, I cast my cares on you in hope that you will sustain me,
for you will never let the righteous be shaken.
Lord, I choose to cling to you;
To depend on you for my strength and joy.

"Do not grieve, for the joy of the Lord is your strength."
-Nehemiah 8:10 NIV

12

I want to seek God earnestly.
I want to earnestly seek God and cling to him.
In the dark places, in the light places, I want to sing praise to God.
I want to lift up my hands and proclaim, 'Jesus is Lord' and be satisfied by Him alone.
He is where my hope comes from.
He is the rock I cling to in any storm.
My feet stand firm in Jesus for he is my refuge and my strength.

You, God, are my God,
earnestly I seek you;
I thirst for you,
my whole being longs for you.
-Psalm 63:1 NIV

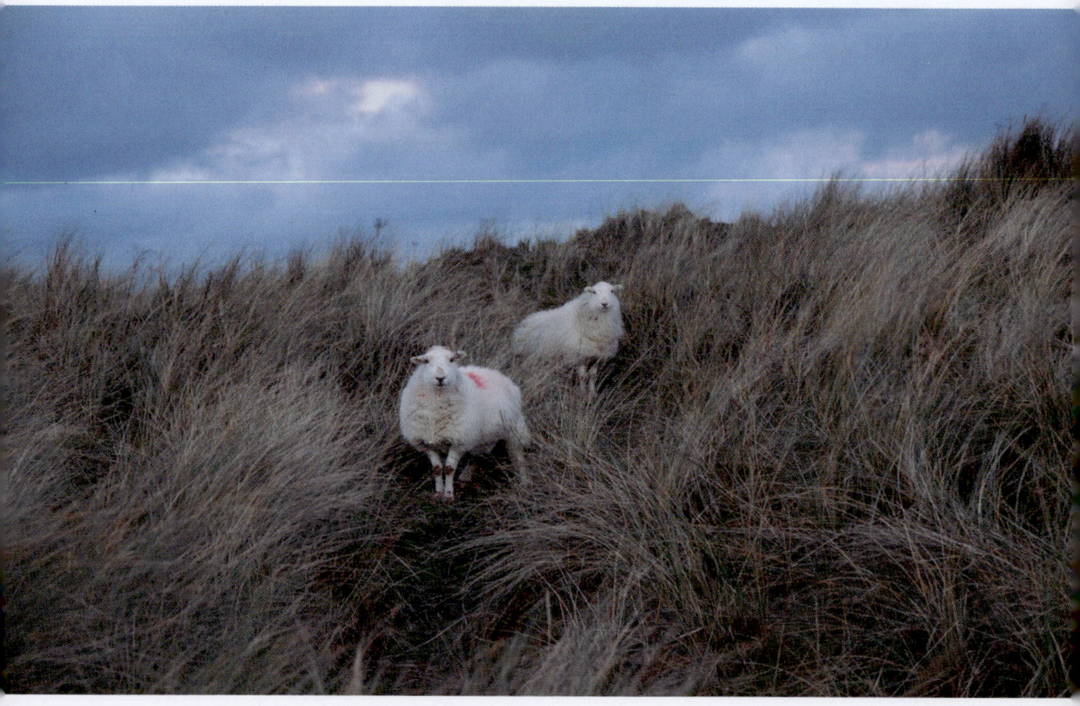

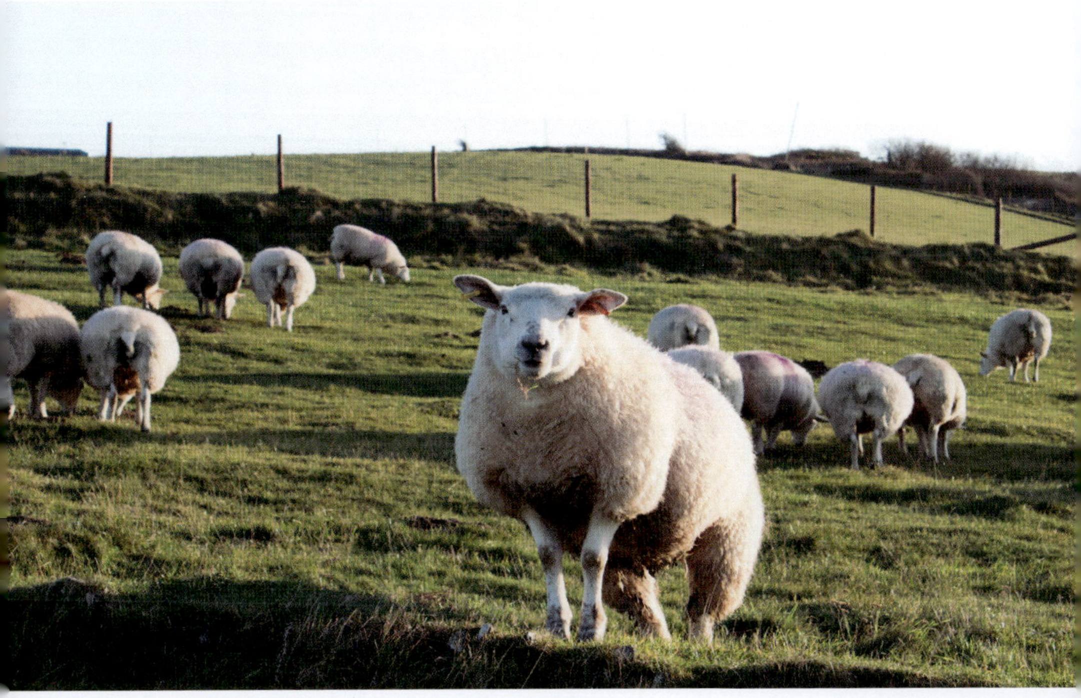

13

O my soul, praise the Lord.
Let everything within me praise his Holy name.
The Lord Almighty who sees all.
He knows my every move.
He knows my every thought.

I pleaded with the Lord to give me strength.
I pleaded with the Lord to give me hope.
I pleaded with the Lord to give me joy.
Hallelujah! The Lord has heard my pleas and answered.

Rejoice and be glad; the Lord has done great things.
Sit and wait in hope.
The Lord has a plan for those things I cannot comprehend;
Wars taking so many innocent lives;
Poverty and financial struggle threaten to take over.
But God is a just God.
God is provider.
God is peace-maker.
Put your trust in him and wait in hope.
Give your concerns to the Lord and he will hold you up.
For those who seek the Lord, He will not let them be shaken.

Rejoice and be glad; the Lord has done great things.

We wait in hope for the Lord; he is our help and our shield.
-Psalm 33:20 NIV

*"For my thoughts are not your thoughts, neither are your ways my ways," declares the Lord.
"As the heavens are higher than the earth, so are my ways higher than your ways and my thoughts than your thoughts."
-Isaiah 55:8-9 NIV*

14

I surrender all.
Lord, you were there before the beginning of time;
You will be there at the end of time.
You are the beginning and the end;
The Alpha and the Omega.
To you, I surrender all.

When my mind is going every which way direction;
When I'm looking for a way out,
I surrender all.
Your plan for my life is way better than my own and in you I trust.
I surrender all.

You fill me with peace as I trust in your plan;
Peace in the chaos;
Peace in the calm;
Peace in the busyness;
Peace in stillness.
To you, I surrender all.

I surrender all.
Lord, you were there before the beginning of time;
You will be there at the end of time.
You are the beginning and the end;
The Alpha and the Omega.
To you, I surrender all.

15

O Heavenly Father, I am not deserving of your grace,
your mercy, your forgiveness.
But I thank you for Jesus who allows me to receive your grace,
your mercy, your forgiveness.

Lord, I need you to cleanse my heart;
humble it and make it new today.
I have had the wrong attitude and have been grumpy.
I need you today.
Please don't let the devil cause me to go in a downward thought pattern spiral.

Father, forgive me and take away the fog and heaviness. Fill me with love, joy, peace, patience, goodness, kindness, gentleness, faithfulness and self-control.

But the Holy Spirit produces this kind of fruit in our lives: love, joy, peace, patience, kindness, goodness, faithfulness, gentleness, and self-control.
-Galatians 5:22-23 NLT

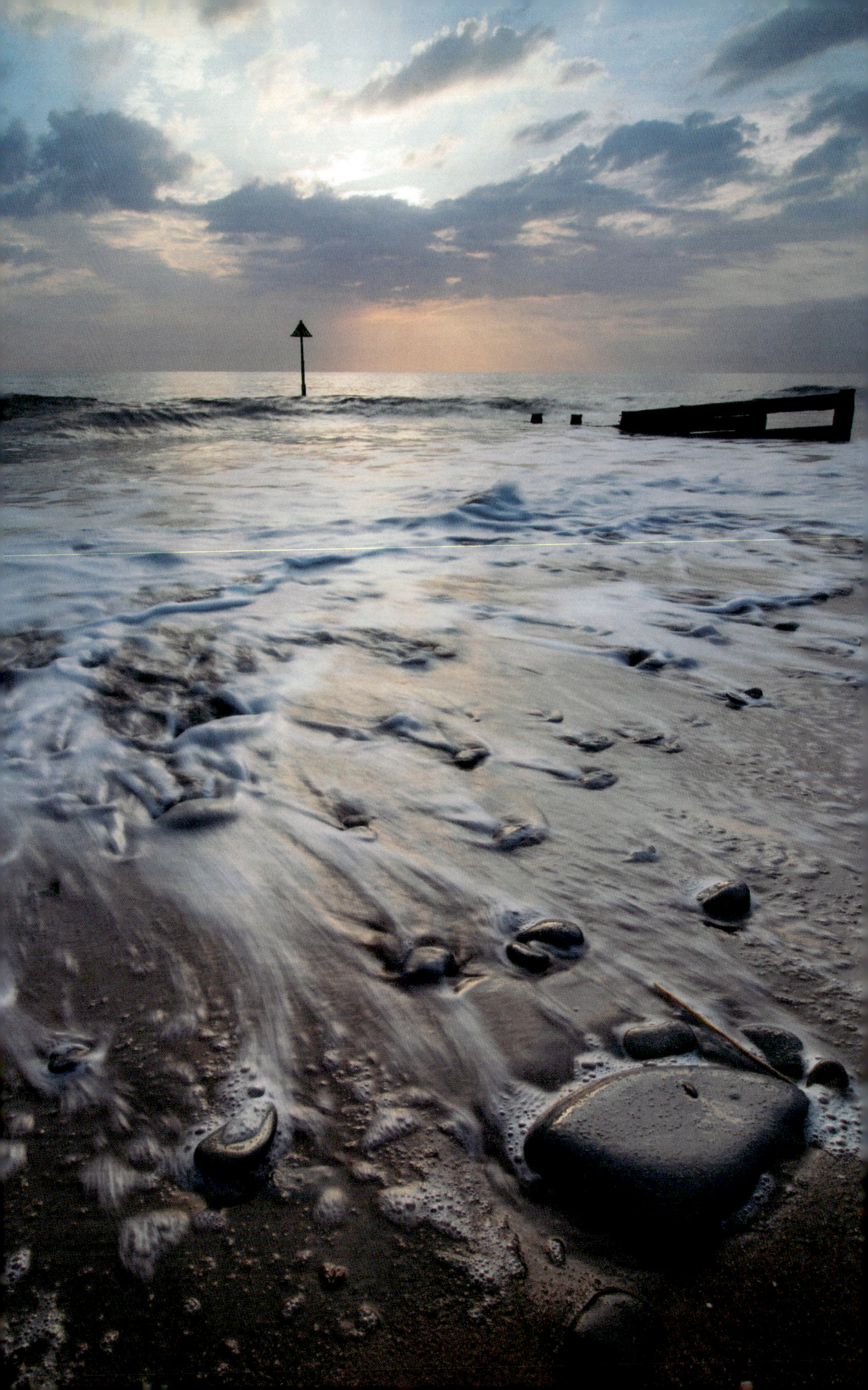

16

By the sea, my soul finds rest.
My naked feet feel the lapping waves gently washing over them.
The bright sunshine reflecting on the water.
The air balmy in the early summer evening.
I find restoration.
I find renewal.
I find strength.
I find hope.
I connect with my Lord and Saviour, Jesus Christ.

It is in moments like these I know it will be OK.
It is in moments like these that the Holy Spirit fills me up with exactly what I need.

Then Jesus said, "Come to me, all of you who are weary and carry heavy burdens, and I will give you rest. Take my yoke upon you. Let me teach you, because I am humble and gentle at heart, and you will find rest for your souls. For my yoke is easy to bear, and the burden I give you is light."
-Matthew 11: 28-30 NLT

17

Jesus, I am angry, frustrated, disappointed.
My spirit feels down and discouraged.

But, Lord, you are good; you have done great things.
I rejoice in you;
I rejoice in you because of all you have done.
In you, I have hope;
I have hope you will strengthen me.
I have hope you will protect me.
I have hope you will guide me.

Give me encouragement when I feel discouraged.
Give me hope when I feel hopeless.
Give me help when I feel helpless.
Give me strength when I feel weak.
Give me grace when I need to give grace.
Give me love so I may love.
Give me peace when all I feel is chaos.
Give me understanding.
Give me sympathy.

Jesus, you are bigger than my circumstances.
I may not know what it is, but you have a plan for me
and in you I trust.

> Rejoice in the Lord always. I will say it again: Rejoice!
> Let your gentleness be evident to all. The Lord is near.
> Do not be anxious about anything, but in every situation,
> by prayer and petition, with thanksgiving, present your
> requests to God. And the peace of God, which transcends all understanding,
> will guard your hearts and your minds in Christ Jesus.
> -Philippians 4: 4-7 NIV

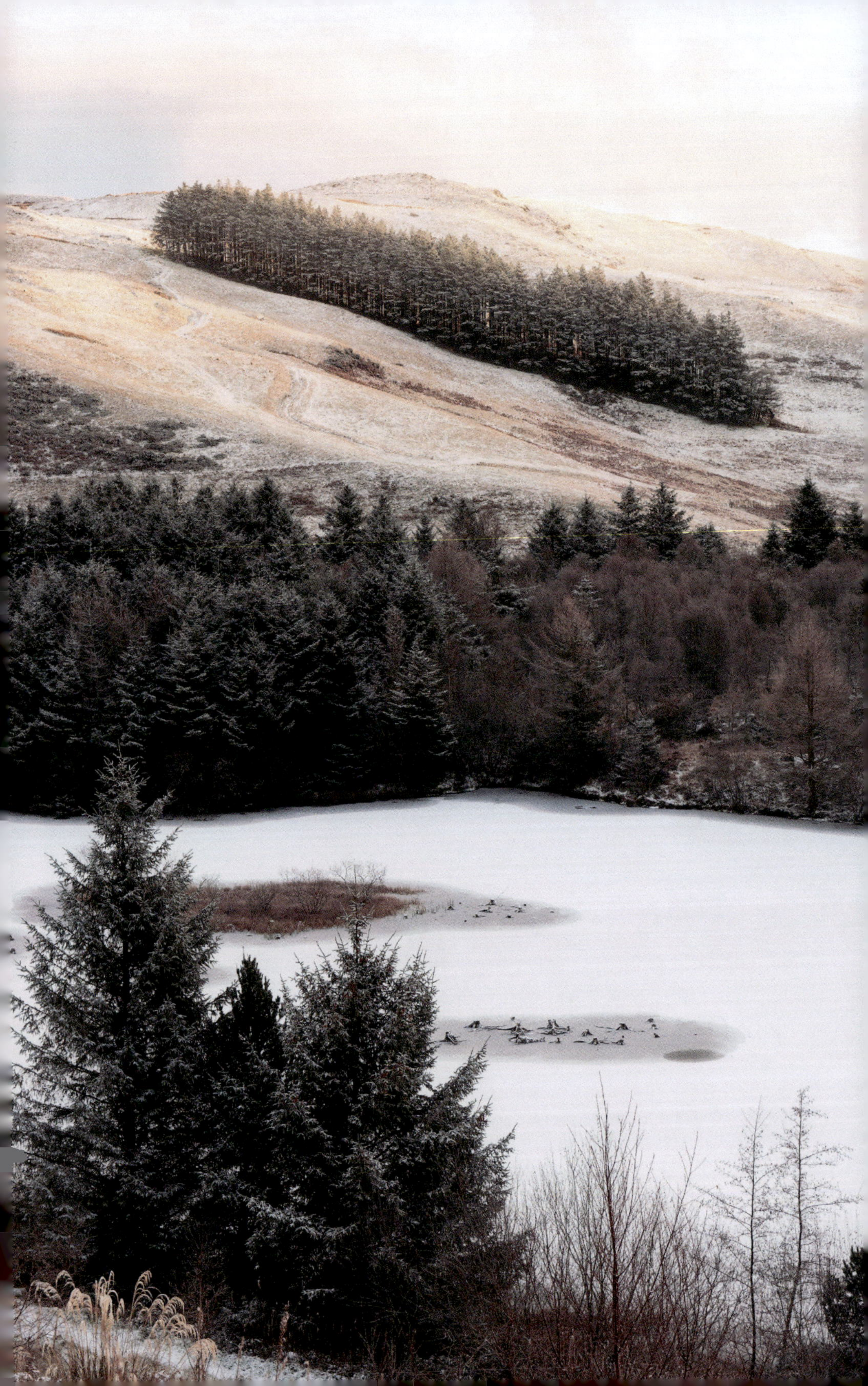

18

Lord Almighty, how wonderful is your name; how powerful you are.
You make the sun rise and set, creating new days.
You pay attention to detail, each fingerprint,
each snowflake, each spiderweb;
a new, unique pattern.

The Lord has compassion on his people.
He is our refuge and our strength.
In times of trouble we can call on his name;
In times of trouble we can call on his name and he will listen.
He makes wars cease to the ends of the earth.
He loves righteousness but despises injustice.
He is bigger than man and the actions man takes.
The Lord will fight for his people.
His people need to be still and know he is God.

Those who have done evil in the eyes of the Lord,
will have to go before God and answer for their actions;
God will deal with them.
Those who look to God will be saved.
Those who fear the Lord will be saved.
We put our hope in the Lord, for He is good.
He will deliver his people and make their enemies fall.
Trust in the Lord always and rejoice in his name.

"The Lord will fight for you; you need only to be still."
-Exodus 14:14 NIV

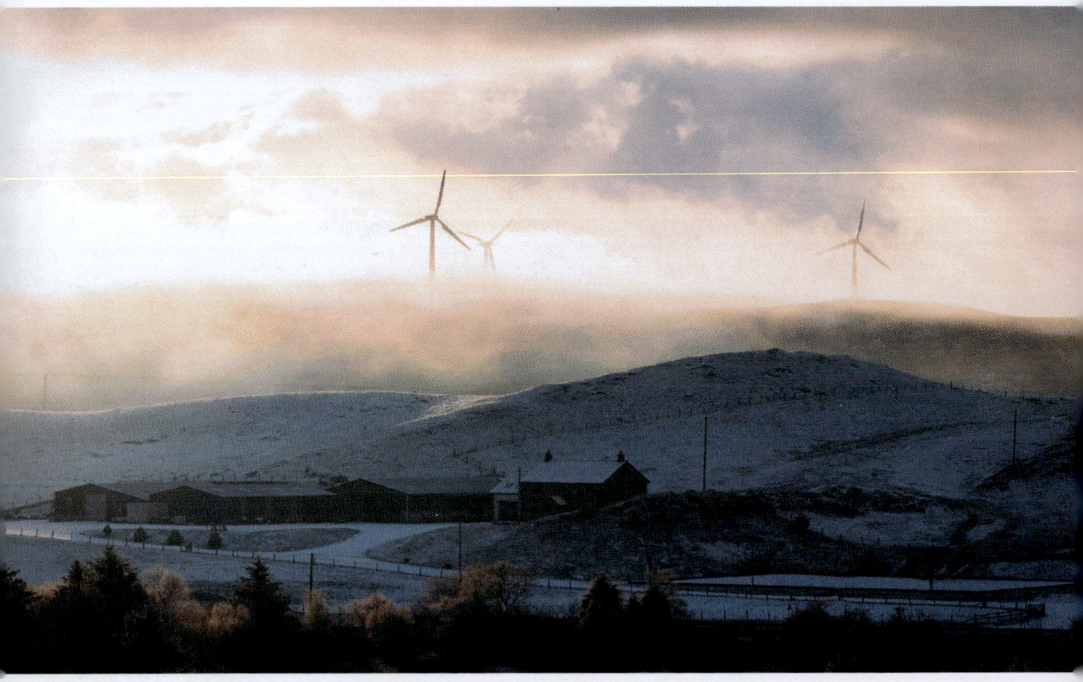

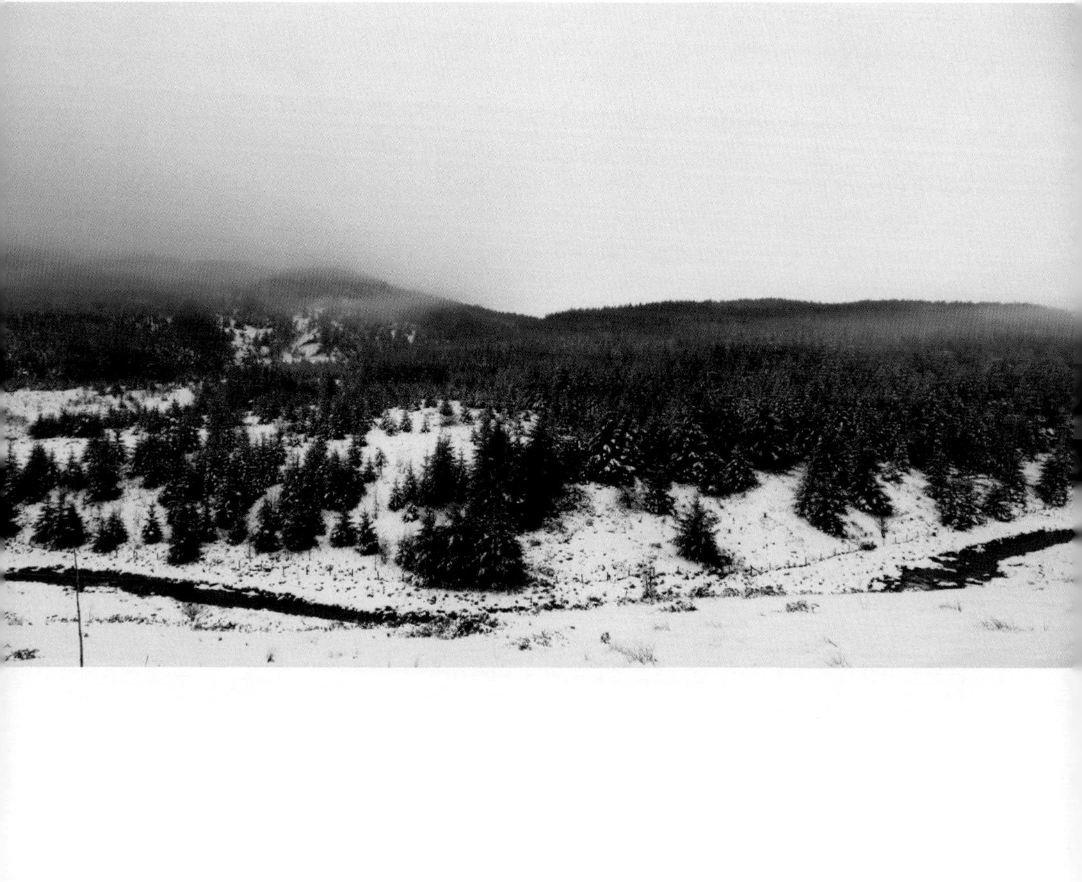

19

O Lord, my soul is downcast, my spirits are low.
I feel under attack for declaring praise to you
but Lord I will not stand for it.
My body longs to lie down and rest.
My mind longs to be free of responsibilities for a little while.
But God, I know you are my refuge;
You are my strength.
I seek you for comfort.
I seek you for wisdom.

Lord, I have not been wise with my decisions
and now I face the consequences.
I run to you for forgiveness, for you are where my salvation comes from.
Lord, grant me wisdom and the strength,
the self-control to do what is wise.
Lord, you are the light of my life;
Without you, there is only darkness.
I stumble around, falling and fumbling, not knowing which way is which.
Lord, you light the way.
With you, life is so much clearer.
O Lord, my soul is downcast, my spirits are low.
I will put my hope in you.
I will praise you all the days of my life.

The devil has no hold over me for you are my victor;
You are my redeemer.
You have, you do and you always will fight for me.
I turn to you, O Lord, for you are my comforter, my refuge.
In you, I find strength;
In you, I find hope;
In you, I find love.

Your word is a lamp for my feet, a light on my path.
-Psalm 119:105 NIV

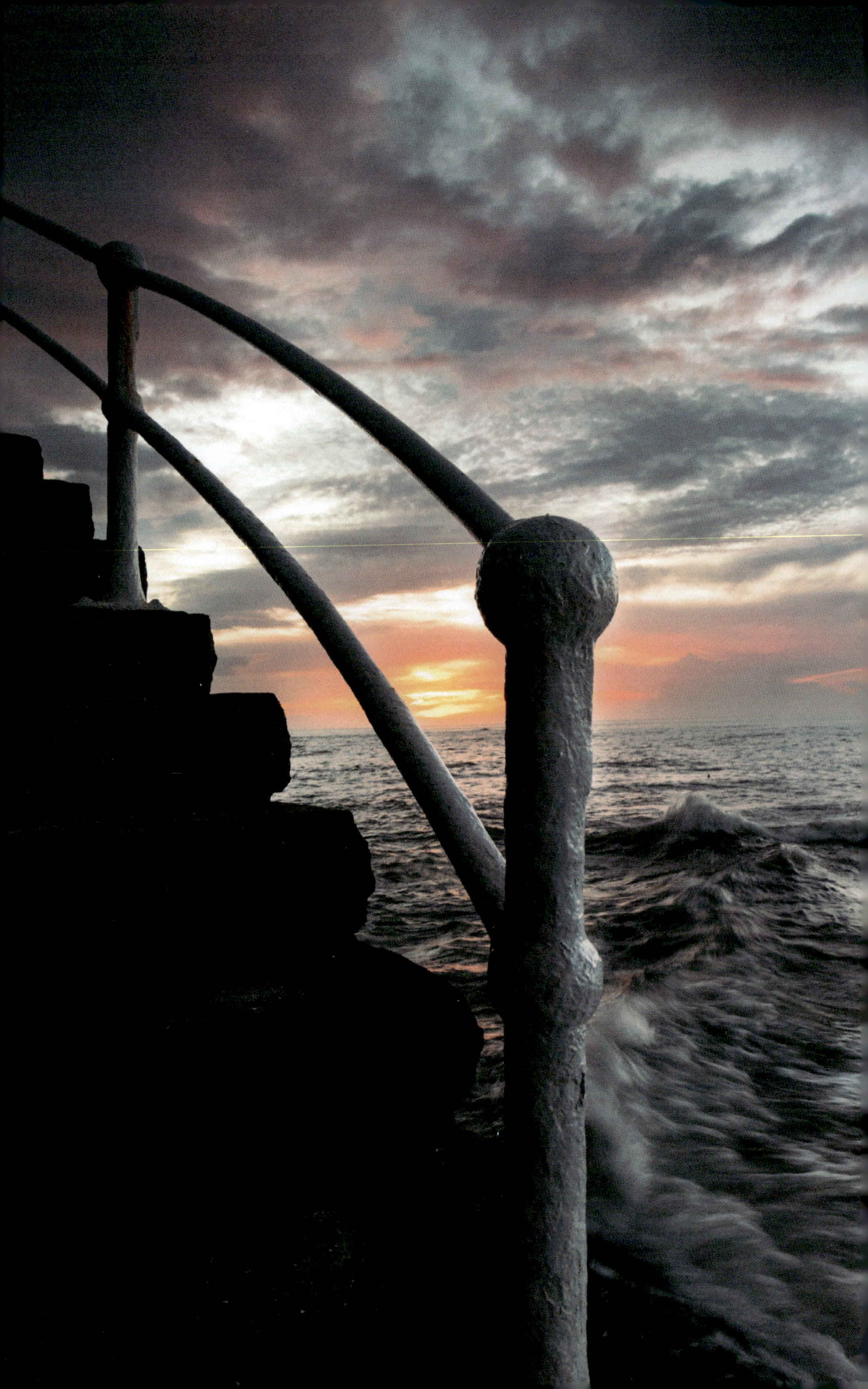

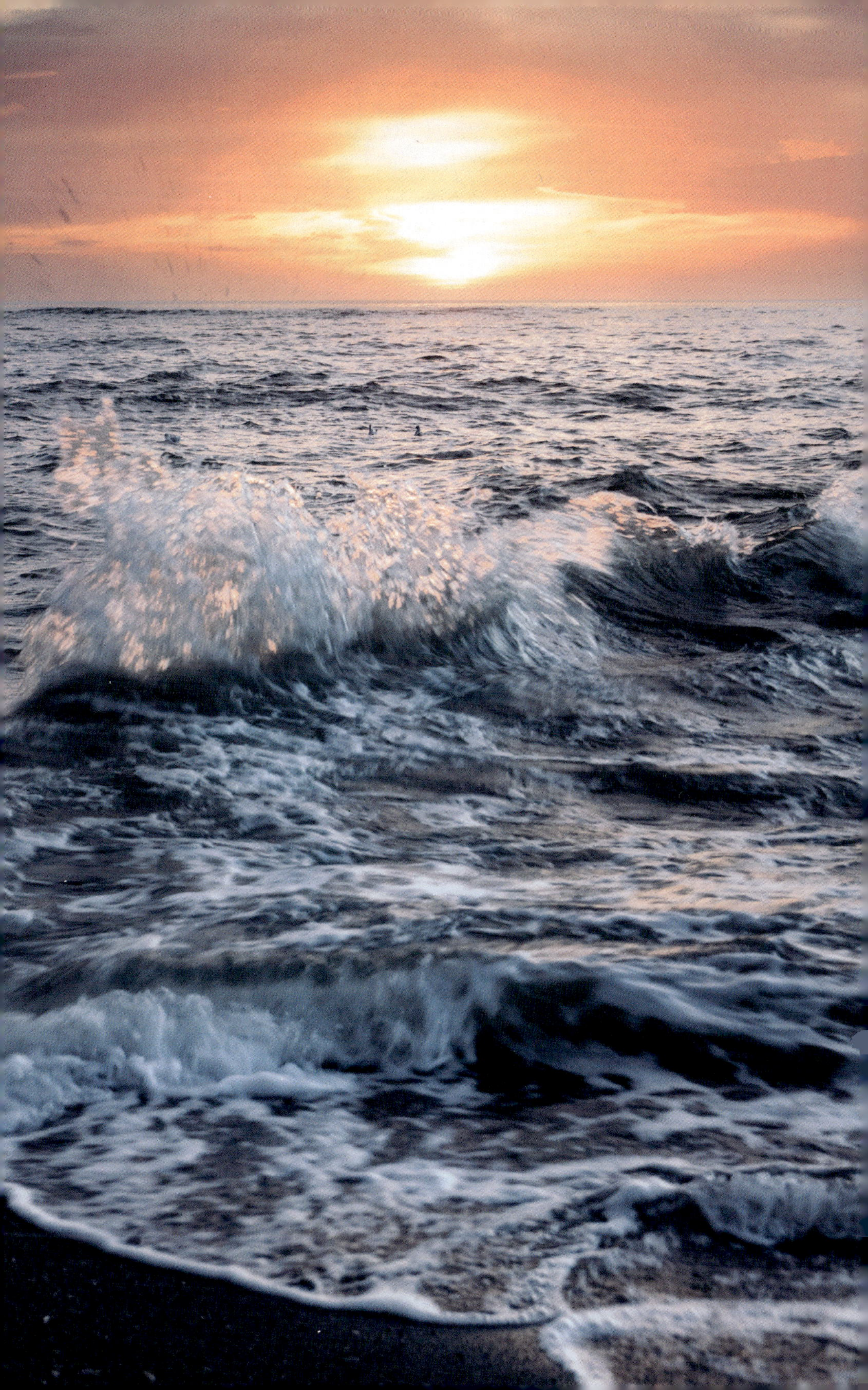

20

Lord, Lord, I long to see your face;
I want to see your hands at work.
You are mighty; you are worthy of praise.
All the days of my life, your praise will ever be on my lips.
You are my rock, my comfort; rest for my soul.
I pour out my cares to you and you listen.
Day and night, you hold me;
You will never let me fall.
My hope comes from you and you will never fail me.

21

I praise you, Lord, from the chair I sit on, the blanket I sit under.
To see you at work is a wonder.
To know you is a joy.
You lavish your love on us and take delight in us.
You give us marvellous things, gifts to enjoy.
May we delight in these things, use these gifts, but most importantly, may we take delight in you, our creator and provider.
Lord, may we seek you earnestly and see you at work.
May our eyes always be open to see you.
May our ears always be open to hear you.
May our hearts always be open to know you.

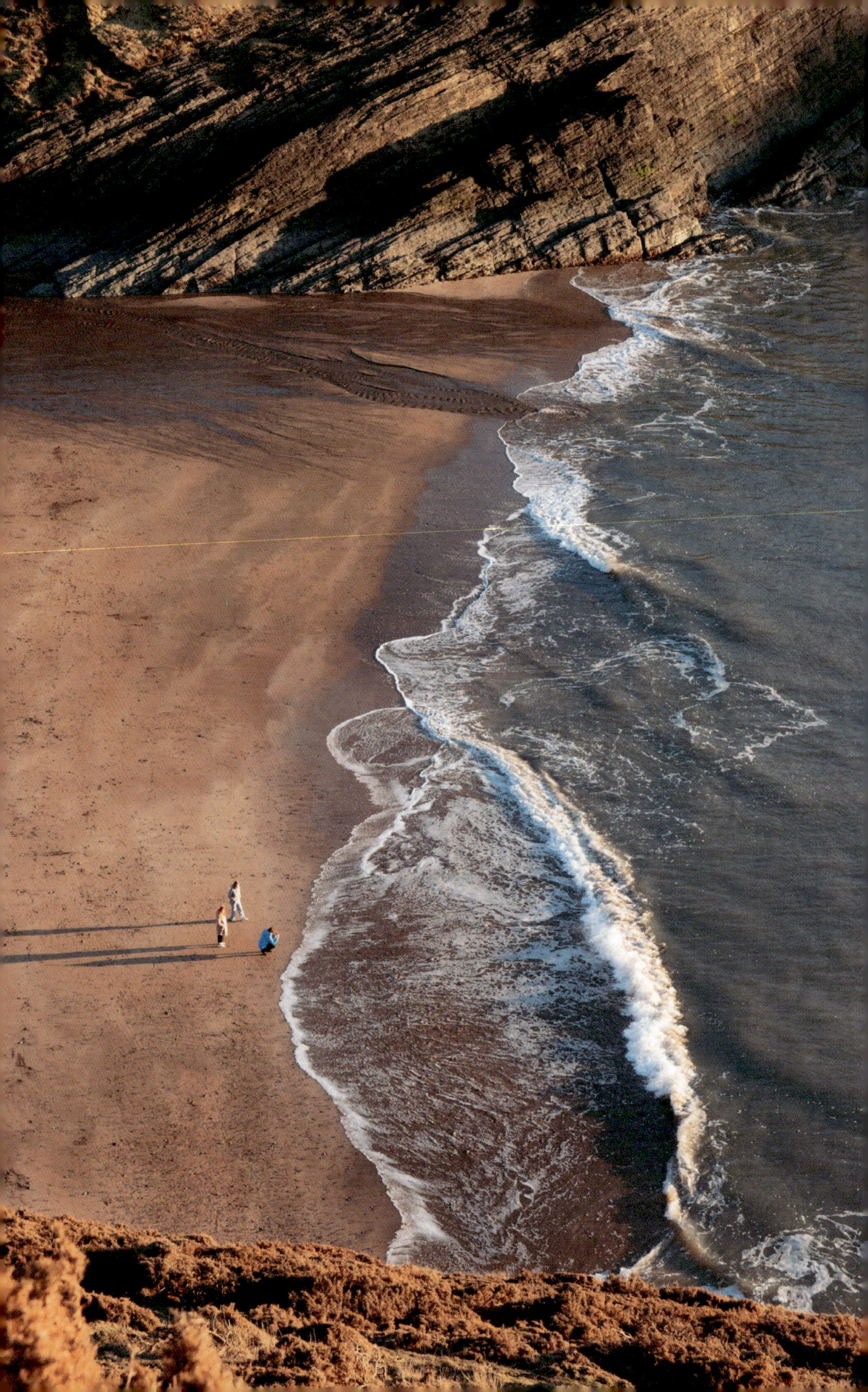

22

Lord, Lord, I praise your wonderful name.
Wherever I go, you are with me;

In the fogginess of my mind, I seek clarity.
In the uncertainty of my soul, I seek peace.
I will not be afraid because you will help me.
Lord, may this truth be known to all your creation.
May your love be shown to all.

Lord, grant the desires of the hearts of those who delight in you.
We do not always know or understand the plans you have for us, but may we always trust in you; our refuge and the rock we stand on.

Take delight in the Lord,
and he will give you the desires of your heart.
-Psalm 37:4 NIV

23

When I feel overwhelmed by the challenges life has thrown my way and I can't see a way forward, I hold onto the promise that you, Jesus will sustain me;
That you will keep me grounded.

It's not easy, Lord but as I try to take each day as it comes, I ask you help me through this day.

I pray today that you fill me with the peace that only comes from you.

I pray that amidst any uncertainties or trials of life, I have peace and am encouraged in the knowledge that you, Lord, have gone before me and will carry me through whatever situation I find myself in.

"I have told you these things, so that in me you may have peace. In this world you will have trouble. But take heart! I have overcome the world."
-John 16:33 NIV

Verses of encouragement

Remember your promise to me;
It is my only hope.
Your promise revives me;
it comforts me in all my toubles.
-Psalm 119: 49-50 NLT

You have done many good things for me, Lord,
just as you promised.
I believe in your commands;
now teach me good judgement and knowledge.
-Psalm 119: 65-66 NLT

Lord, sustain me as you promised, that I may live!
Do not let my hope be crushed.
Sustain me, and I will be rescued;
then I will meditate continually on your decrees.
-Psalm 119: 116-117 NLT

Cast your cares on the Lord
and he will sustain you;
he will never let
the righteous be shaken.
-Psalm 55:22 NIV

But may all who search for you
be filled with joy and gladness in you.
May those who love your salvation
repeatedly shout, "God is great!"
-Psalm 70:4 NLT

I pray that God, the source of hope, will fill you completely with joy and peace because you trust in him. Then you will overflow with confident hope through the power of the Holy Spirit.
-Romans 15:13 NLT

I pray that from his glorious, unlimited resources he will empower you with inner strength through his Spirit. Then Christ will make his home in your hearts as you trust in him. Your roots will grow down into God's love and keep you strong.
-Ephesians 3:16-17 NLT

In his kindness God called you to share in his eternal glory by means of Christ Jesus. So after you have suffered a little while, he will restore, support, and strengthen you, and he will place you on a firm foundation. All power to him forever! Amen.
-1 Peter 5:10 NLT

The Lord is good, a refuge in time of trouble.
He cares for those who trust in Him.
-Nahum 1: 7 NIV

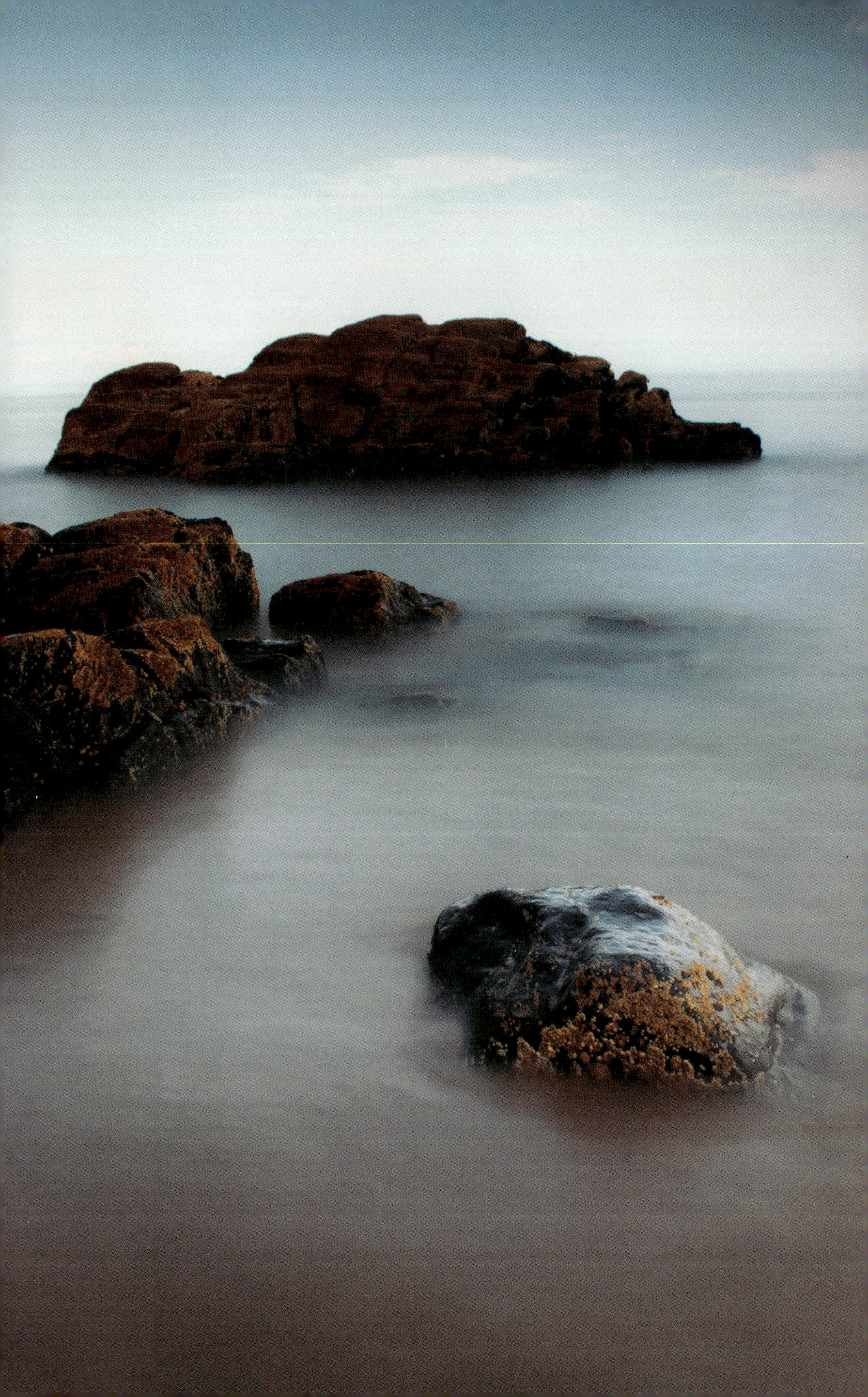

Part Three
Truth & Creativity

Creative Beings

We are made to be creative.

I truly believe that since we are image bearers of the one true God, and that God is a creative God, we as humans are made to create.

Nothing brings me more joy than arriving at a beach at golden hour, with my camera and knowing I get to capture that beauty.

Nothing brings me more joy than letting the words of praise flow into poetry and songs of worship fill my heart as I connect with my maker.

The words in this next section are the outpouring of inspiration found when in God's creation and I can sit and be still and know that he is God.

He says, "Be still, and know that I am God.
-Psalm 46:10a

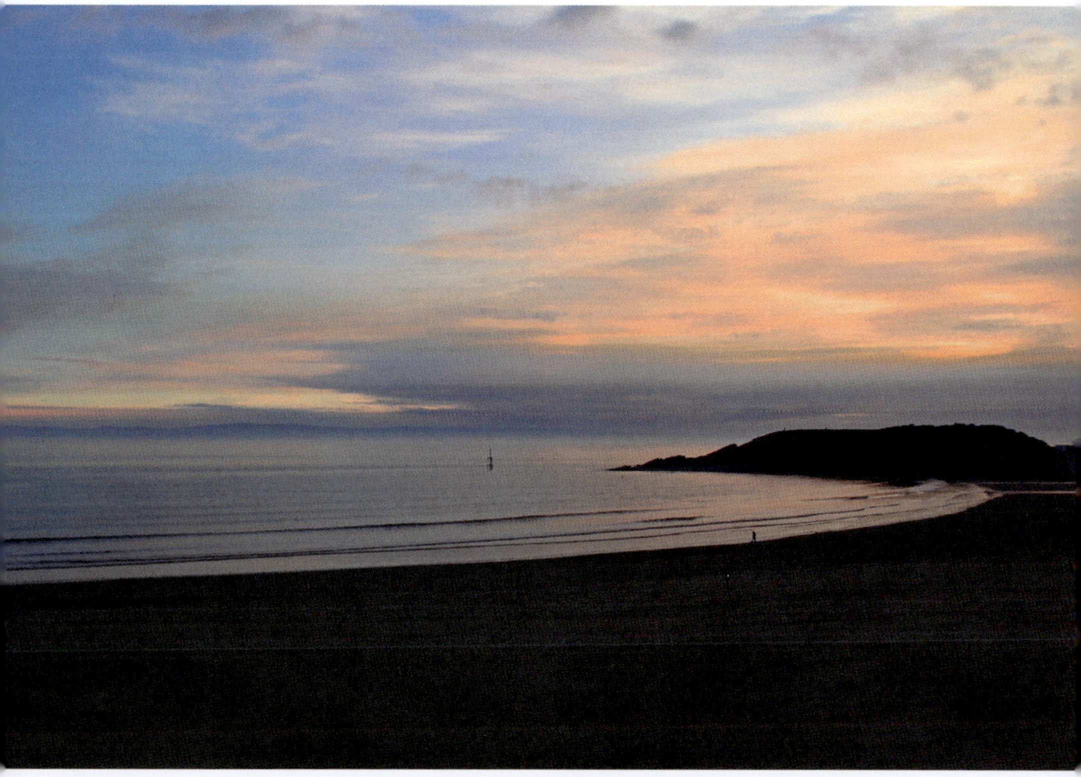

24

We are made to be creative.

We are made in the image of God and God is the original creator. He is the master of creation.
To be creative is to worship.
To be creative is to be free.

Remember this; being creative is more than being top of the class. It is more than creating the perfect piece.
It is as much about the journey as it is the final product.
The final product is but one piece of the puzzle.

Allow yourself to be bad, rubbish, not very good.
Allow yourself to write nonsense, to draw an unrecognisable picture;
Do an uncoordinated dance;
Experiment with a new recipe even though it may end up inedible.
Enjoy being creative.
Enjoy doing it for yourself, for Jesus.

Remember also, not all your creations need to be for the public eye.
Write that novel.
Draw that picture.
Take that photo.
Let the words write themselves.
Let the pencil move around the page.

Don't think too much.
Don't criticise.
Just do.
Just be.
Let go of your preconceptions and create.

25

There is something about being by the sea.

Something breathtaking.
Something awe inspiring.
Something calming.

I stand and look out to sea.
I notice the waves crashing against the harbour wall.
The surfers riding the dusky waves.
The pinkiness of the sky as the sun sets on yet another day.

Then I look around and notice someone else doing as I am doing.
Standing. Just standing, looking out to sea.
We both find a rock and sit.
Really, there is nothing to see but an empty, cloudless sky and the movement of the sea.
Yet, we can't help but sit and just stare at the vast view before us.

The sound of the sea is thunderous.
The sound of rocks rolling into the sea as the waves pull them back in.
Large waves rise and fall as they crash on the sea shore.

My soul finds rest and I feel a calm within.
A joy rising within me.

There is something about being by the sea.

Something calming.
Something awe inspiring.
Something breathtaking.

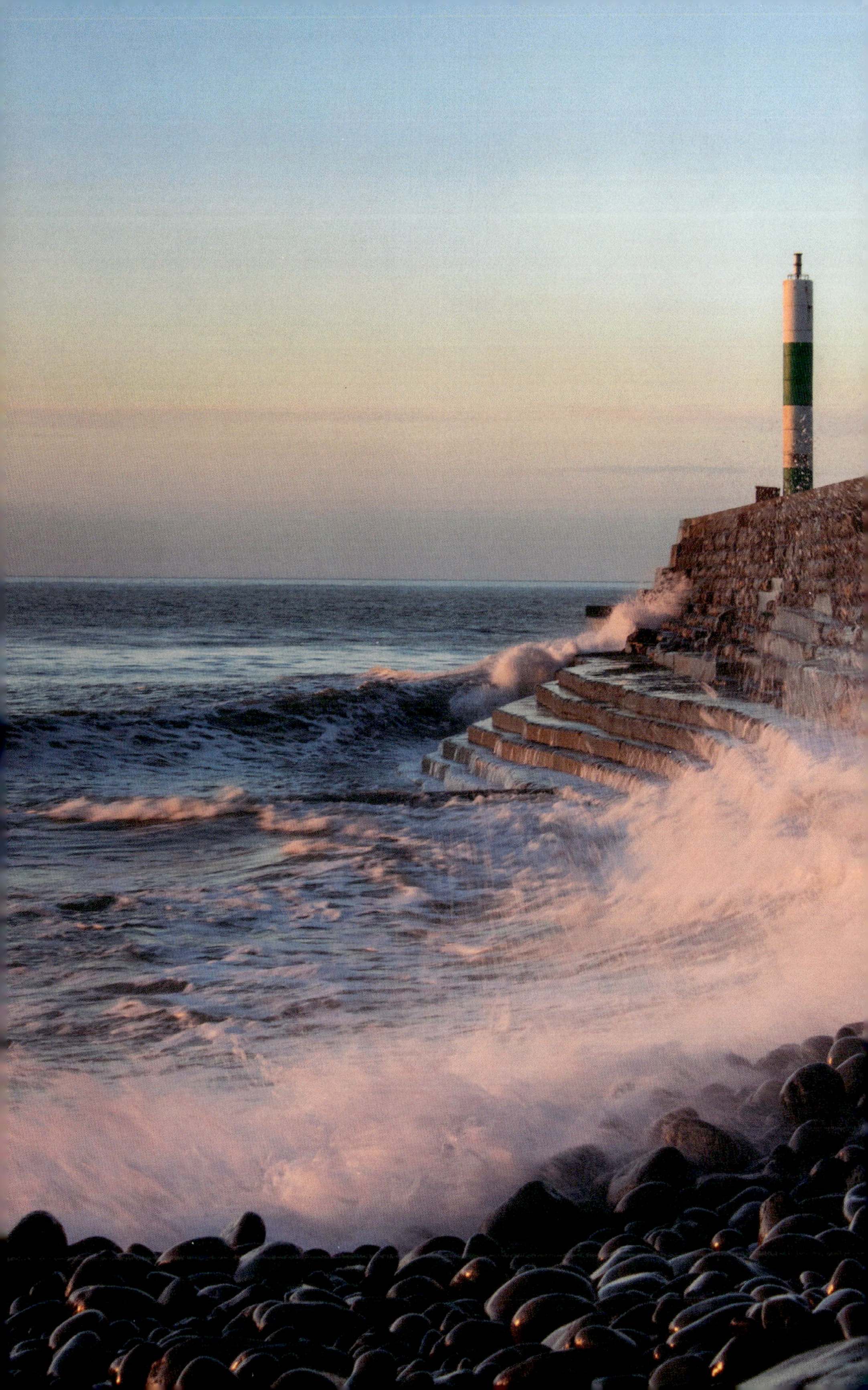

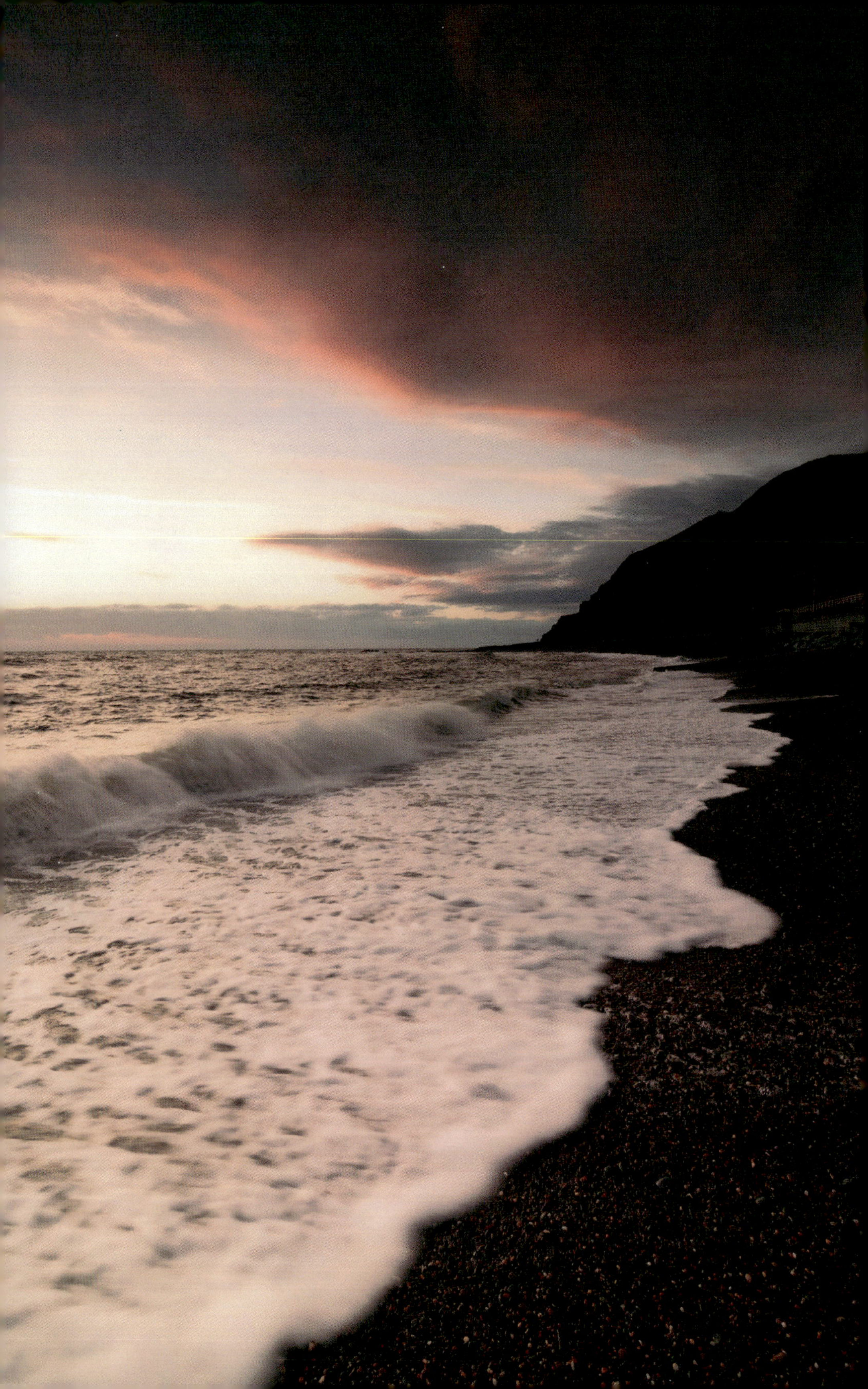

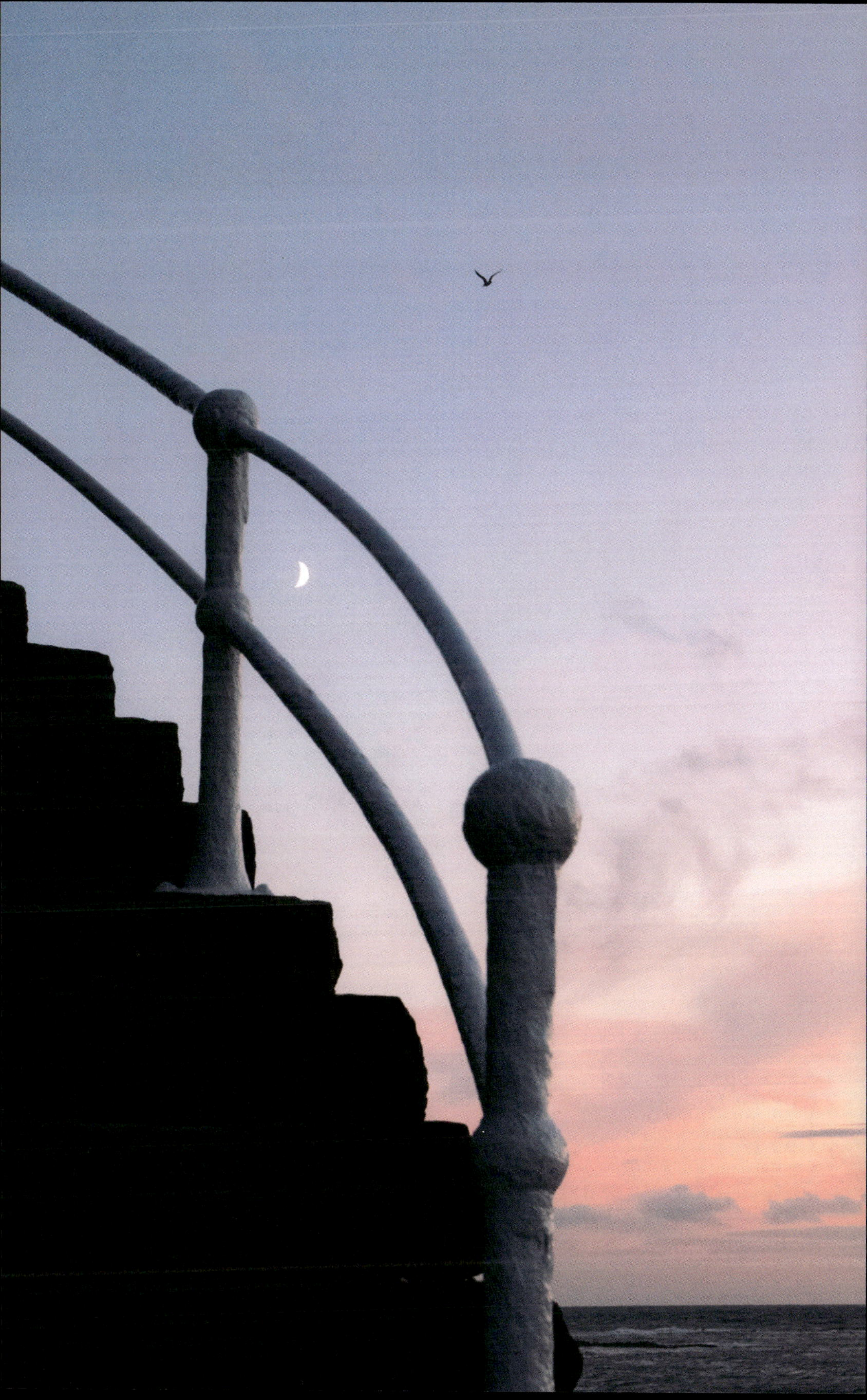

I have come that they may have life, and have it to the full.

-John 10:10b NIV

26

Breathe. Inhale. Exhale.
Let go of the stresses weighing you down and give them to Jesus.
Ask the Lord of peace to fill you with life-giving peace.
In your tiredness and weariness, ask the Lord to restore you.
Jesus came so that you may have life in abundance.
With Jesus, you can live in more than survival mode.

Sit. Be still in the presence of God.
Soak in the Holy Spirit.
Take a moment to prepare yourself for the day ahead and ask Jesus to equip you with what you need to live life fully.
Breathe. Inhale. Exhale.

Just breathe.

27

I sit. I listen. I watch.
The skies above me are blue; not a single white cloud to be seen.

I sit. I close my eyes. I breathe.
The birds happily singing their merry tune.

I sit. I watch. I take in.
The snowdrops, with all their delicacy, dancing in the sunlight.

I sit. I listen. I close my eyes.
All my worries, in that single moment, disappear.

I sit. I ponder. I appreciate.
Spring awakening, bringing hope of a future with life.

I sit. I listen. I watch.

*"Forget the former things;
do not dwell on the past.
See, I am doing a new thing!
Now it springs up; do you not perceive it?"*
-Isaiah 43:18-19a NIV

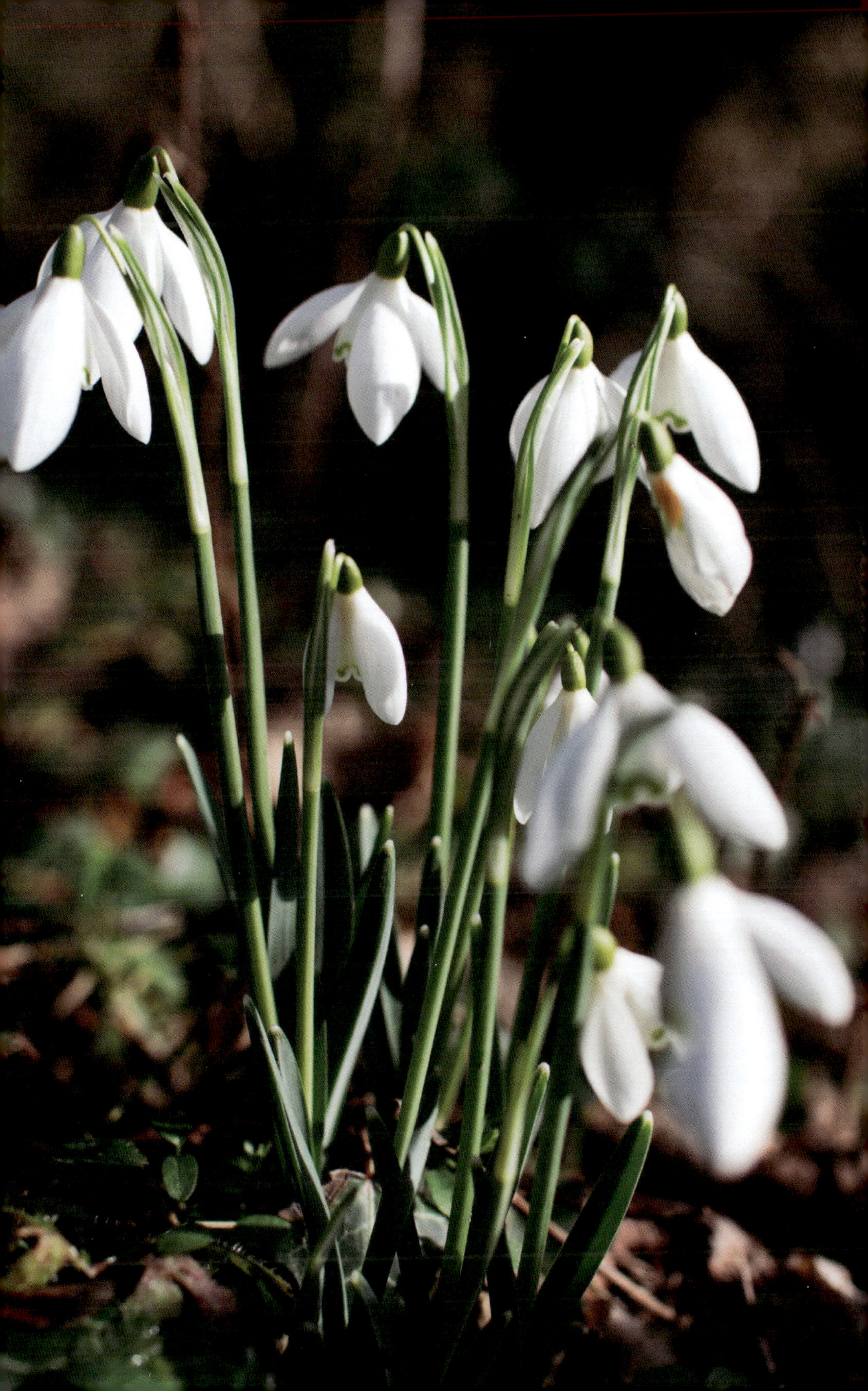

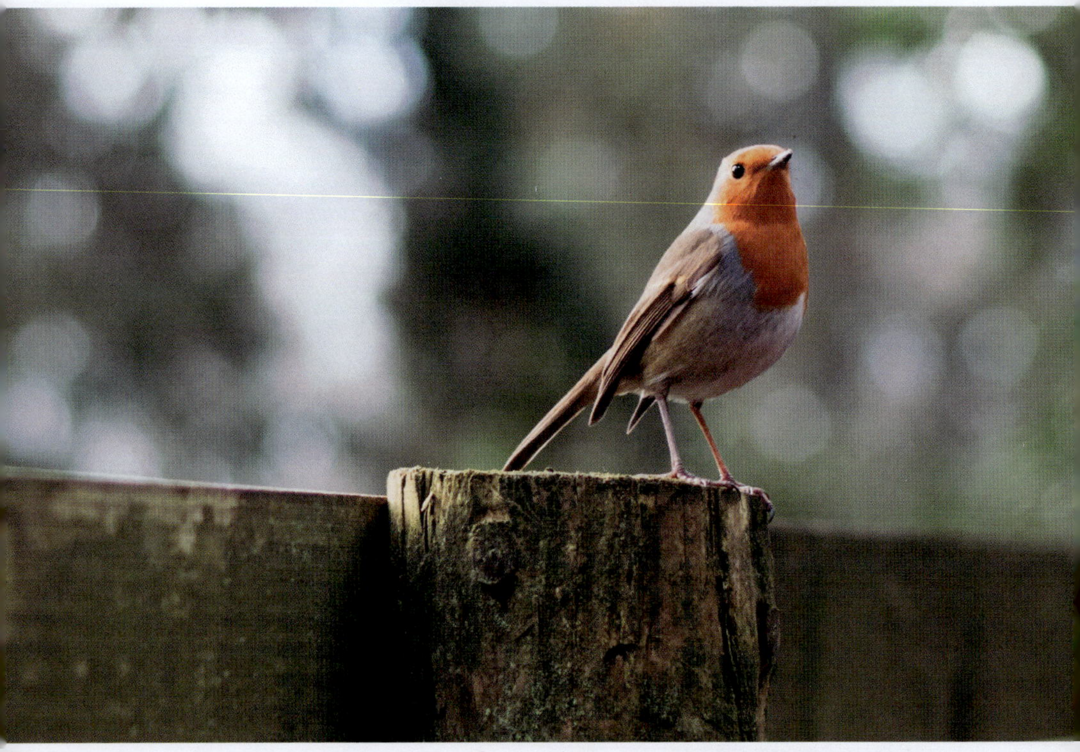

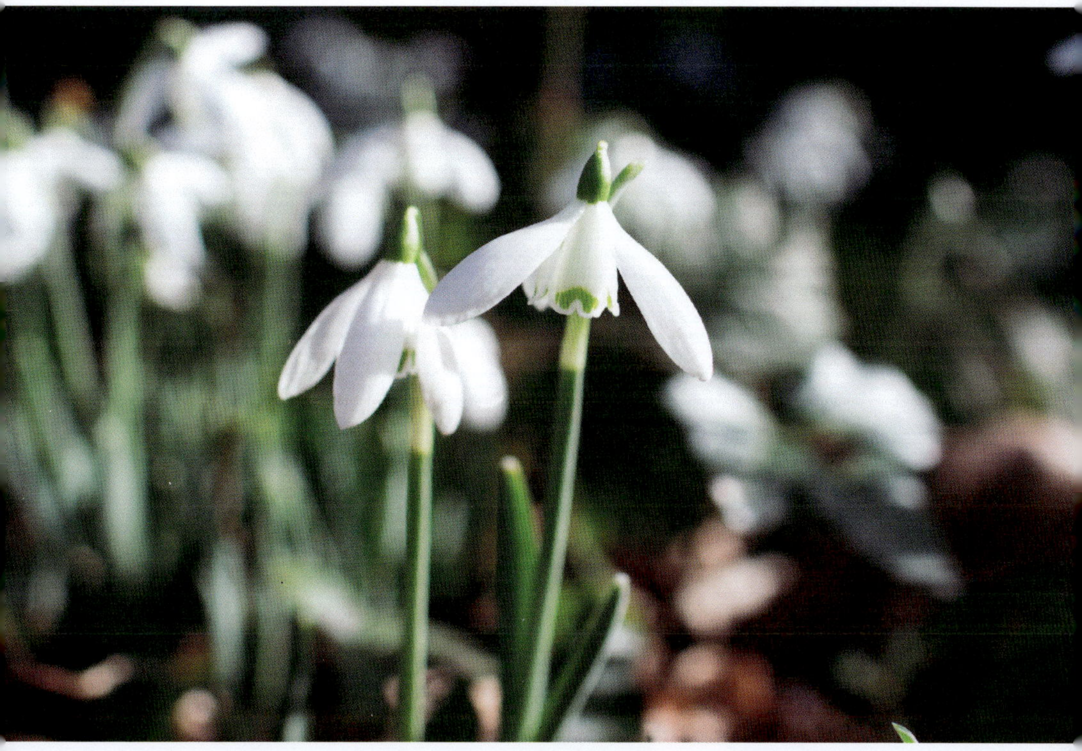

28

God wants us to tell him our concerns.
He wants to take that burden away from us.
Not necessarily by changing our circumstances
but by carrying us through it;
by sustaining us.

He doesn't want to let us be uprooted by our circumstances but rather give us the strength to stand firm in him.
So come, share your burdens with God.
Let Him carry you through.

> *Cast your cares on the Lord and he will sustain you; he will never let the righteous be shaken.*
> *-Psalm 55:22 NIV*

29

Don't doubt your prayers and requests - instead, be expectant.
Be expectant that God will answer.
Be expectant that you will see God working.

What good is it to pray and then immediately doubt?
We pray in faith and hope and expect Jesus to move.

In the morning, Lord, you hear my voice;
in the morning I lay my requests before you
and wait expectantly.
-Psalm 5:3 NIV

30

God is faithful; this I know to be true.
God is good; this I know to be true.
God is provider; this I know to be true.

Life is busy, it's chaotic, it's messy.
Life is wonderful, it's beautiful, it's simple.
Life is seasonal.
Yet as seasons change there is always one constant - Jesus.
Jesus is the same yesterday, today and forever.

Some seasons are easy, simple, beautiful and some are not.
Some seasons are hard, exhausting and trying.
But seasons do not last forever.
In difficult seasons Jesus gives us peace. He is with us in every season.

Let your heart take courage and wait on the Lord.
Difficult seasons do not need to lead you to packing up your home and leaving.
Difficult seasons do not need to lead to you handing in your resignation.
Difficult seasons give the opportunity to lean into God, find refuge and strength in Him.

There is nothing too big for God to handle.
When you're exhausted, go to Jesus.
When you're overwhelmed, run to Jesus.
When you want to scream and shout, pour out your heart to Jesus.

Bring the chaos, the mess, the pain and lay it at Jesus' feet.
Bring the beauty, the wonder, the simplicity and sing praise to Jesus.

No matter what season you find yourself in, God is faithful, God is good, God is provider.
God is with you in all seasons of life - walk with Him.

Jesus Christ is the same yesterday and today and forever.
-Hebrews 13:8 NIV

*Truly my soul finds rest in God;
my salvation comes from him.
Truly he is my rock and my salvation;
 he is my fortress, I will never be shaken.
-Psalm 62: 1-2 NIV*

31

I sit.
I inhale.
I exhale.
Watching the waves of the evening tide lap over the rock on the shoreline.
My soul finds rest.

I sit.
I inhale.
I exhale.
Waiting for the break of the wave to be in perfect position for me to click the shutter button.
My soul finds rest;
My soul finds rest in the beauty of God's creation.

I sit.
I inhale.
I exhale.
The sea a silvery, silky body of movement.
There is no magnificent display in the sky this evening but oh how it is beautiful.
So calm. So serene.

I sit.
I inhale.
I exhale.
My weary soul finds rest.
My downcast spirit is lifted within.

I sit.
I inhale.
I exhale.

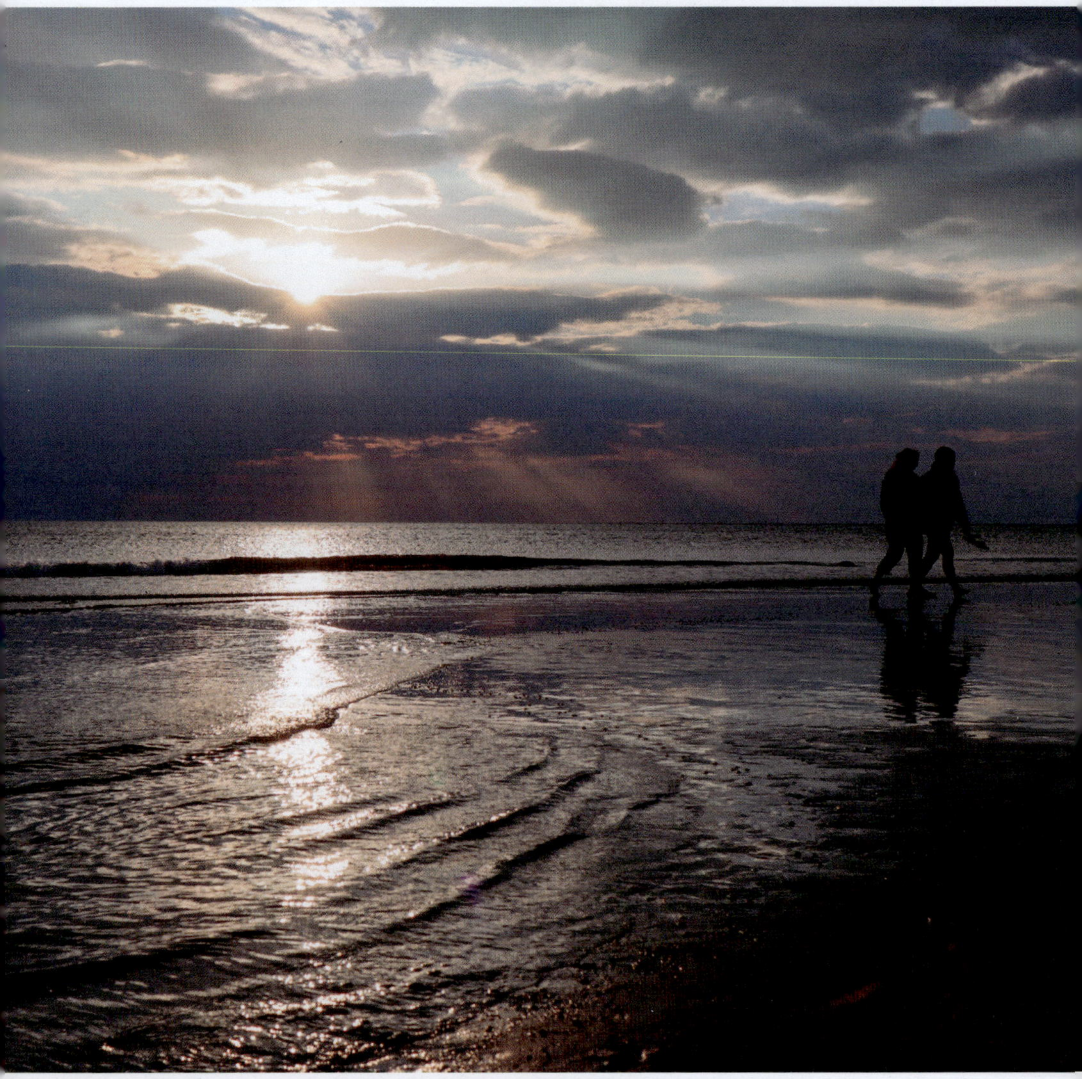

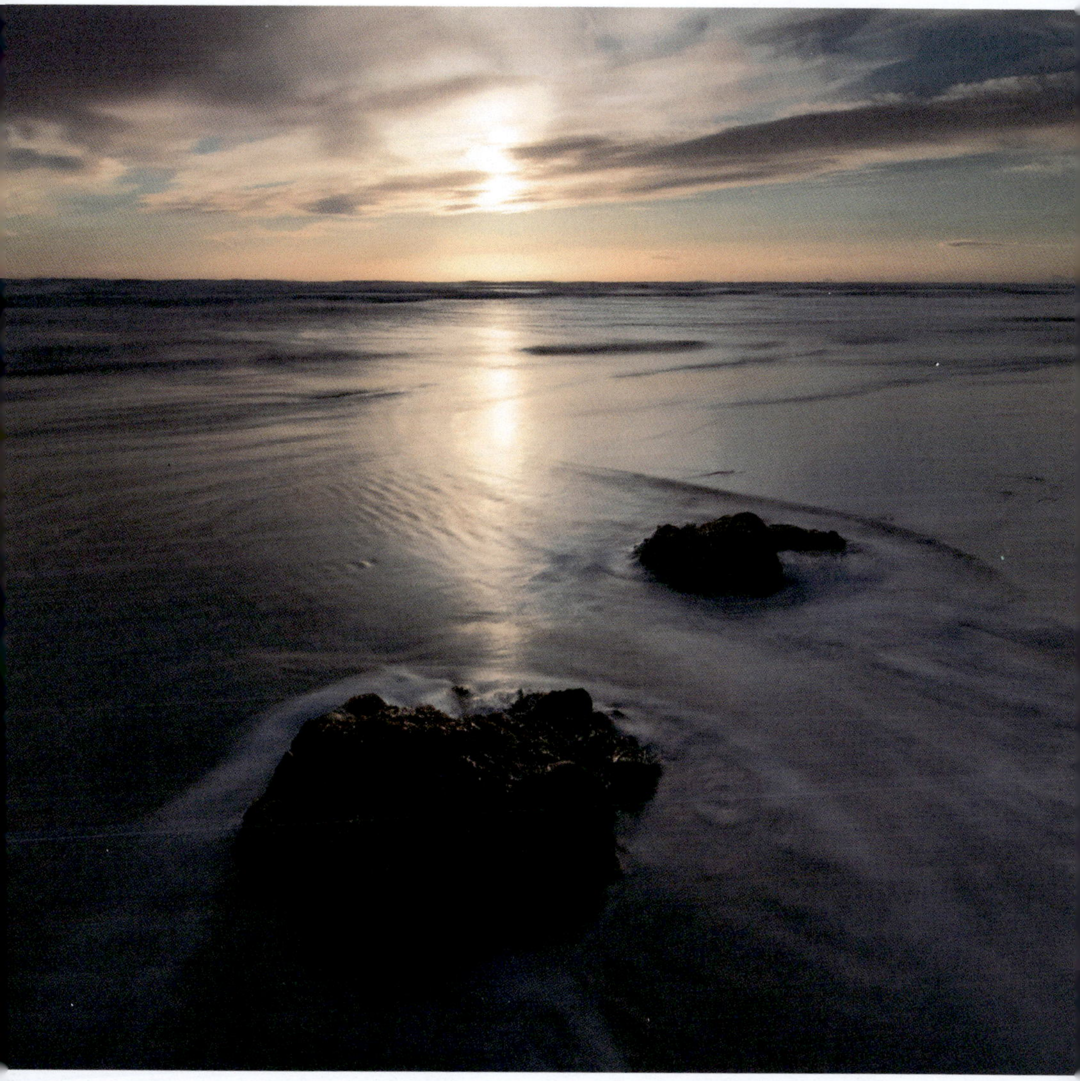

32

We have no reason to fear.
God tells us not to be afraid because He is with us;
Not to be scared because He holds us in His right hand.

We have no reason to fear because through Jesus' victory on the cross, we are conquerors.
In fact, we are more than conquerors and absolutely nothing can separate us from the love of God.
If God is for us, who can be against us? No-one!
How amazing is that!?

Jesus, when He made us, did not give us a timid, fearful spirit but a spirit of power, love and self-discipline.
God does not want us to be afraid.

Verses that hold this truth:
Isaiah 41:10
Romans 8: 31, 37
2 Timothy 1:7

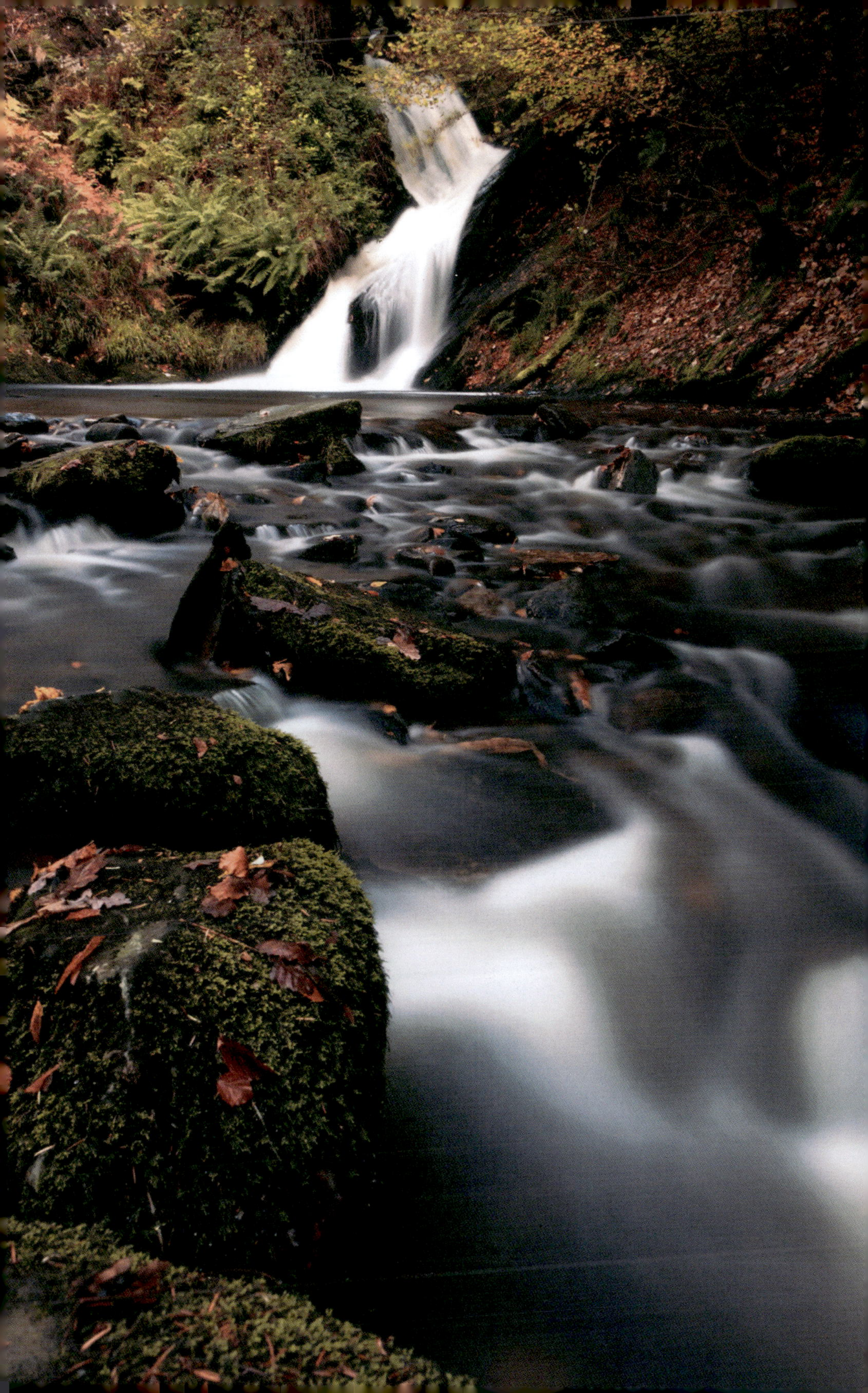

33

All my weariness, my fears and my failures fade into nothing in comparison to the simple beauty I see around me;
The vastness of the sea;
The golden morning sun lighting up the houses of the harbour;
The stillness of the early morning;
The fluffy cloud formations;
A lone surfer sitting, waiting to catch the next wave.

It is in that moment I realise how much love the creator of those beauties has for me.

It is in that moment I know He has got it all sorted.

It is in that moment I have a sense of clarity.

It is in that moment I am inspired.

It is in that moment I realise I need more of those moments.

To be in the moment, to enjoy and appreciate all that is around me.

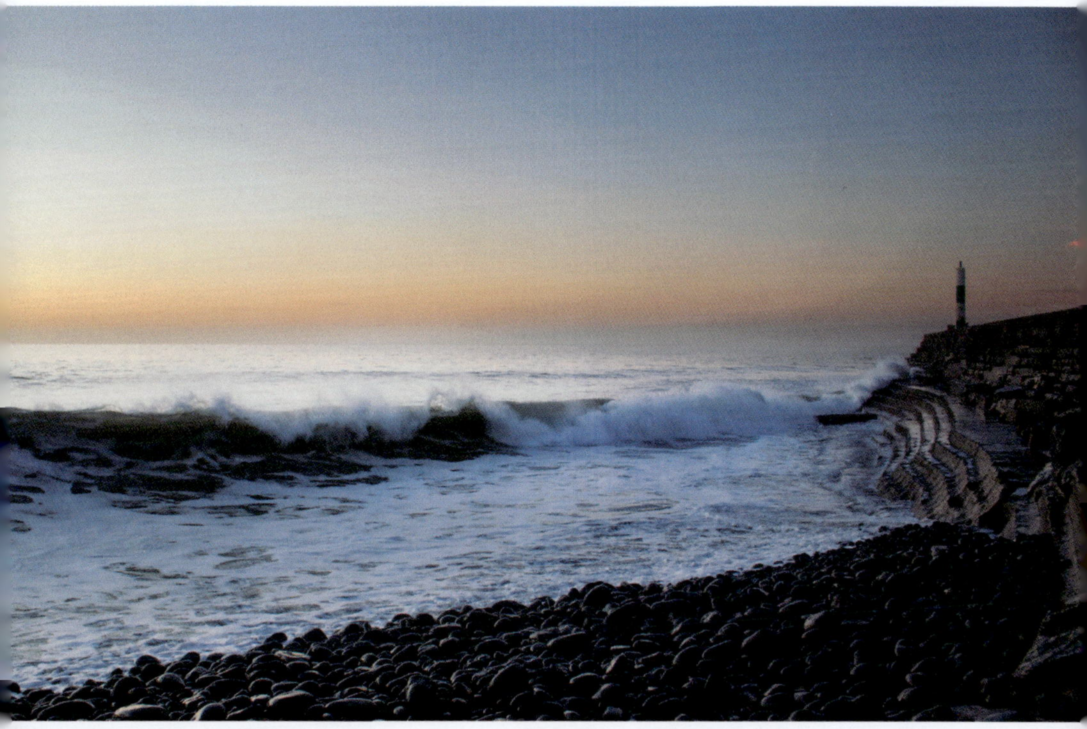

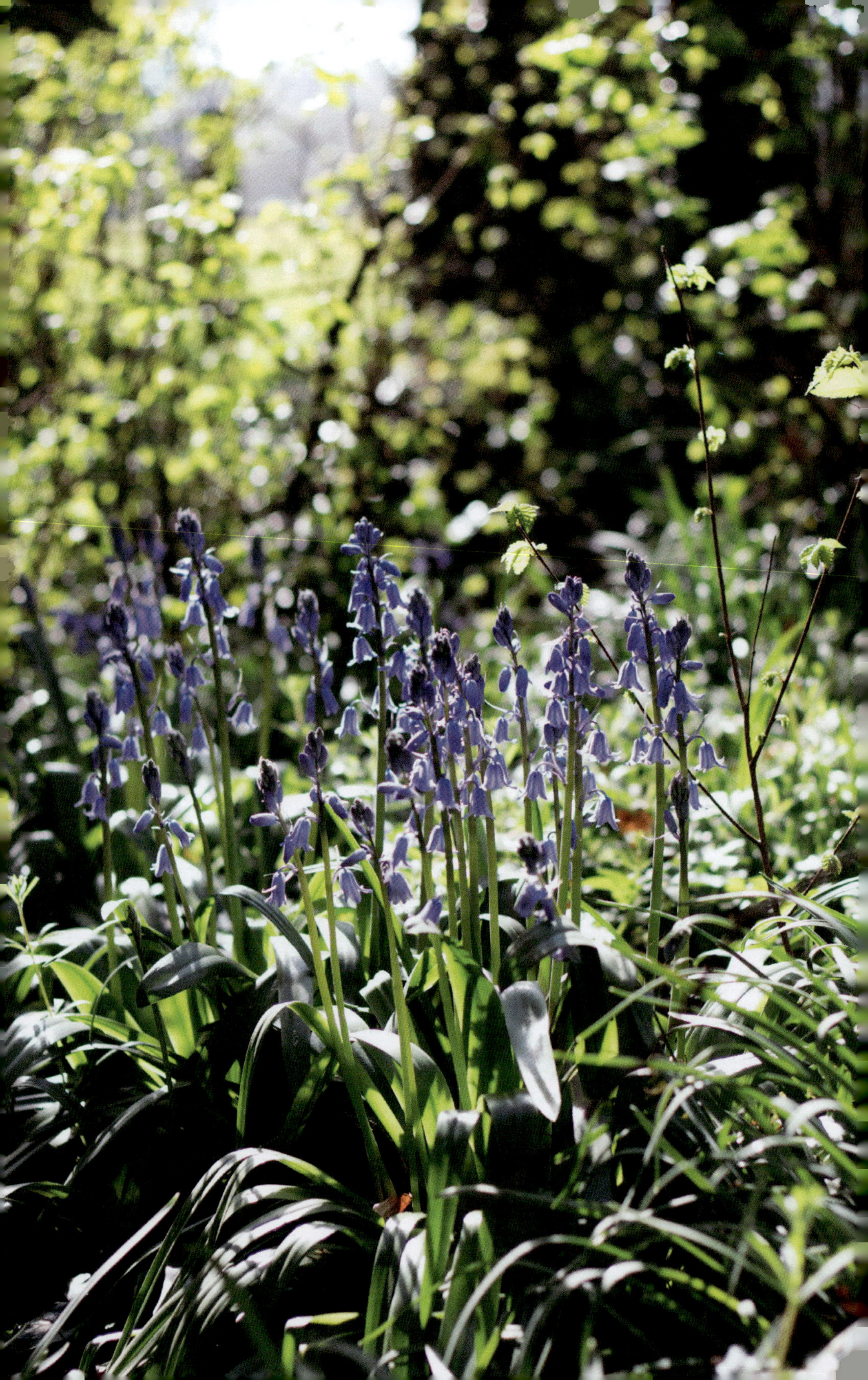

34

I sit.
I close my eyes and turn my face towards the sun.
Oh, how it feels warm.
The gentle breeze blowing loose strands of hair around my face.

I can hear the birds singing.
A woodpeckers' call.
The other birds I cannot identify, yet I long to know;
To learn.

I hear the laughter of a young boy who finds his Mumma after circling the house on his bike.

I sit.
I take it all in;
Willing the sunshine to stay for as long as possible.
The shift in seasons bring hope and optimism;
It brings joy and productivity.
Things feel brighter, lighter, somehow.

I think about the horrific things going on in the world;
Things too big for my mind to comprehend.
Then I hear my Father's voice whisper;
'They are not too big for me. I am in control.
Enjoy these small, simple moments.'

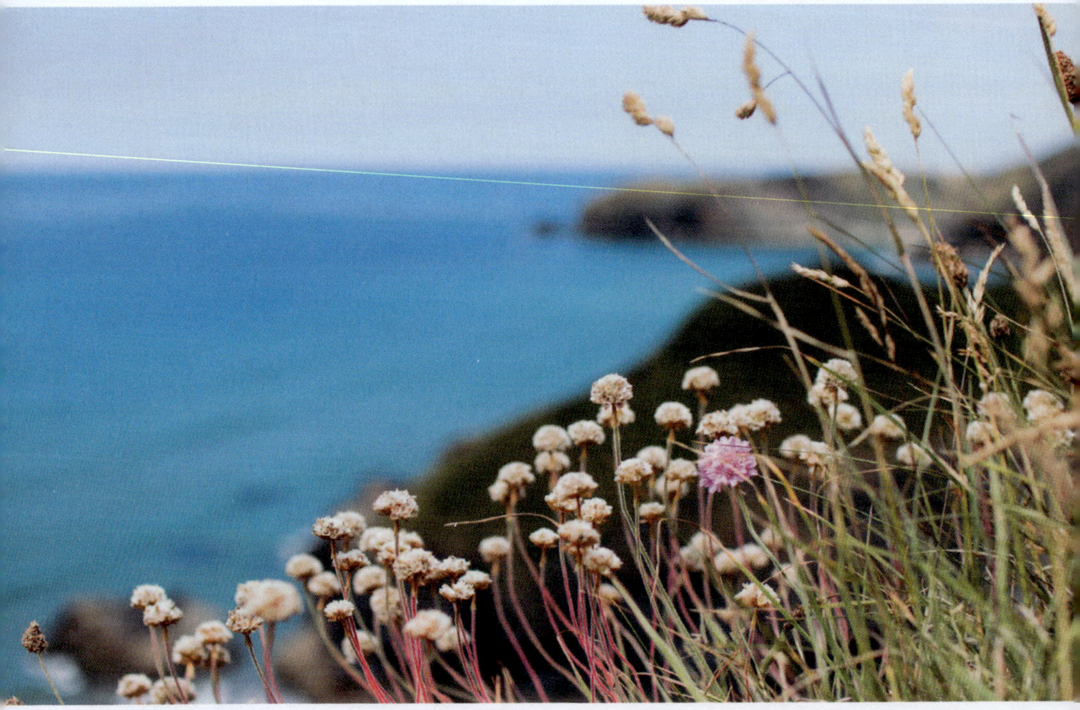

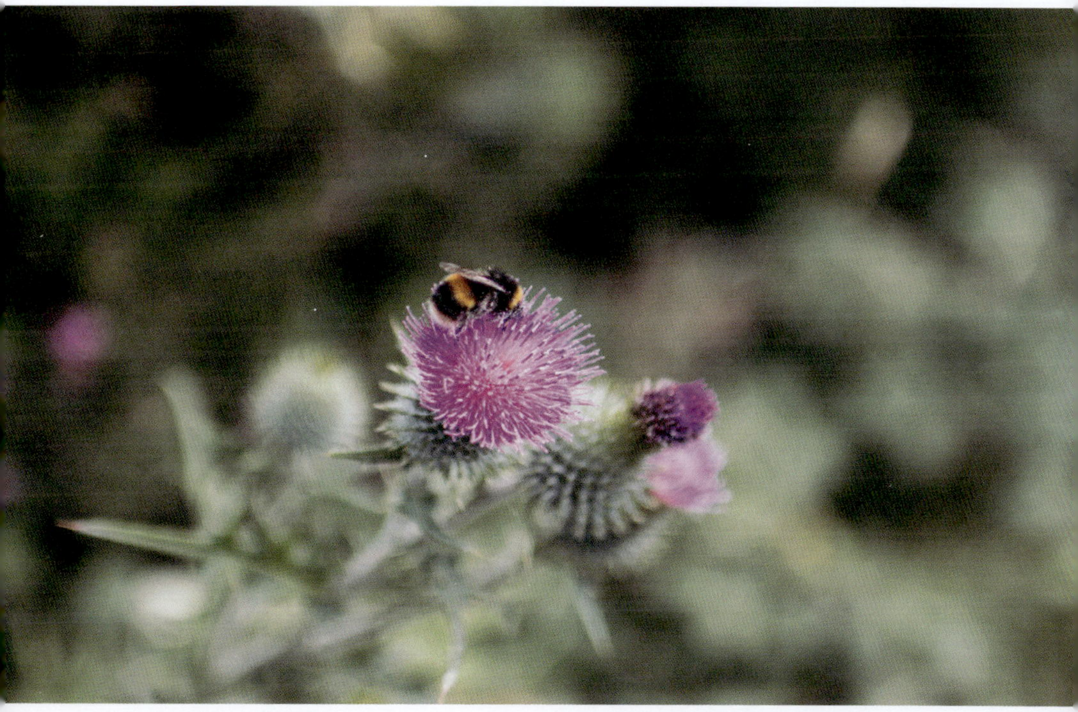

35

God chose you before the world began.
He wanted you to be on this earth right now
and He made that happen!
You are His creation;
His masterpiece;
how can you not love that truth?
Why don't you believe it?
God has amazing plans for you.

You have a purpose, works created by your Heavenly Father for you to do.
God loves you so incredibly much, with an everlasting love.
Believe it.

Let God fill your heart with His love and abundant joy.
Allow yourself to feel and better still, allow yourself to know this truth and joy in your heart.
Allow yourself to grasp how wide, long, high and deep the love of Christ is;
Know this love that surpasses all knowledge
 so that you may be filled to the measure
of all the fullness of God.
He is able to do immeasurably more than you could ask or imagine.
Believe this truth also.

He is far bigger than your issues.
In fact He has overcome your issues.
While you will have trouble on the earth, you can take comfort in knowing Jesus has overcome it.
He leaves peace with you.

You can live life through faith in the Son of God who has loved you and gave himself for you!
You can come to Him in confidence because He has overcome everything.

And because of this, your story matters.

You matter!

Verses that hold this truth:
Ephesians - All of it
Jeremiah 29:11
Jeremiah 31:3
John 16:33
Galatians 2:20

Final Words

No matter what is going on in life, Jesus remains constant and if we seek him, we will find strength and true joy; not a fleeting feeling of happiness, but deep joy and peace in the knowledge that Jesus has gone before us and walks with us through our difficulties, through our pain.

My prayer for you and this book is that you found encouragement, hope and a little inspiration to seek God, to find some strength and to be filled with joy and gladness in him.

Acknowledgements

To my husband, Sam. Your encouragement and faith in me to 'just do it' led me on a journey in creative writing. I love you and am so thankful for your love and faith in me.

To my boys, Toby and Ezra, for always giving me a challenge. You always light up my day and I will always love your cuddles and kisses.

To my mum, dad and sisters who are always an encouragement in my photography. Thank you for introducing me to the place where I fell in love with watching sunsets and being by the sea. I love you always.

About the Author

Bethan is a mum to two small boys who runs a Bed and Breakfast in Mid-Wales with her husband and also works part-time for the church she attends.

When time allows, she can be often be found with a camera in hand. She loves her morning rhythms of time spent with Jesus, in his word, and journalling.

Bethan is author and photographer for her blog, Capturing Simple Beauty, writing about faith, family days out and sharing her photography.

Printed by Amazon Italia Logistica S.r.l.
Torrazza Piemonte (TO), Italy